Tulliallan: Four lads o' pairts

Biographies of Sir James Wylie; Sir James Dewar; Robert Maule, J.P.; Sir Robert Maule

By Rev. William Meiklejohn, M.A.

1st Edition, prepared MMXIV

ISBN: 978-1-291-83114-6

1

"**Tulliallan: Four lads o' pairts**: *Sir James Wylie, Sir James Dewar, Robert Maule J.P., Sir Robert Maule*" was originally researched and written by Rev. William Meiklejohn, M.A and first printed in 1990 by How & Blackhall, 77 Marygate, Berwick-upon-Tweed.

It was subsequently transcribed and edited for electronic and on-demand publishing in 2014 by Colin Anderson.

Rev. Meiklejohn has dedicated this work:

"To the dear memory of my Father and Mother,

D.M. and E.L.M.

who did justly, loved mercy and walked

humbly with their God.

(Micah VI, v. 8)

In gratitude and love."

Contents

Preface 4

Sir James Wylie 7

    Biography.. 9

    Notes 46

    Appendices... 57

    Interviews with Sir James Wylie - 1854 70

    Through Russian Eyes 74

    Sir James Wylie's Will 78

    The Alexander Legend.. 83

Sir James Dewar 85

    Some Of The Honours Conferred Upon Sir James Dewar
.... 87

    Biography... 91

    Notes 178

    Additional Notes 186

    Absolute Zero... 187

    Tribute By The Royal Institution 188

    Grand Discovery 191

    Liquid Air for Export.. 192

Robert Maule, J.P and his son Sir Robert 193

    Biographies 194

    Notes 236

Preface

Kincardine-on-Forth in Scotland has a long and illustrious history as a river crossing and trading port. This book provides comprehensive biographies of four of its most famous sons:

Sir James Wylie (1768 - 1854) was surgeon to the three Czars of Russia, organiser of the Russian Army's medical service, and founder of the Medical Colleges of Moscow and St Petersburg.

Sir James Dewar (1842 - 1923) was President of the Chemical Society and Fullerian Professor of Chemistry at the Royal Institution (a post held previously by Michael Faraday). He was the first person to liquify oxygen and inventor of the Dewar flask, later commercialised by Thermos as the Thermos Flask;

Robert Maule J.P. (1832 - 1901) and his son **Sir Robert** (1852 -1931) were successful entrepreneurs who established and ran 'Maules', one of the most successful early department stores on Edinburgh's famous Princes Street. Today the location of their Edinburgh store is home to House of Fraser.

This project was a labour of love for Rev Meiklejohn and it is worth noting his research for it was carried out during the 1980s, long before the World Wide Web made it possible to discover such information from the comfort of home. The information collected here is the result of the countless hours

Rev Meiklejohn spent in libraries, archives, and other information repositories around Scotland and elsewhere.

Upon his death in 1997 the copyright for his work was generously donated to Kincardine-on-Forth Local History Group (www.kincardinehistory.co.uk) in the hope that it might help raise funds for community history projects.

When it came to making Rev Meiklejohn's work available electronically I decided it would be quicker in the long run to re-type it rather than rely on Optical Character Recognition. I began the process in 2000 but since it was a 'spare time' project it took until August 2005 to publish Sir James Dewar's biography on the History Group's website, and another five years after that to finally finish transcribing the rest of the text. I think it's fair to say that in many ways the transcription and publishing of this book for modern formats has been almost as much a labour of love for me as Rev Meiklejohn's original work for him.

100% of proceeds from this book go to Kincardine Local History Group. The group is a non-profit community-run organisation whose aim is to research, preserve, and promote the town's history for the benefit of future generations. By purchasing this book you are directly supporting the preservation of Kincardine's local history for the people in the town as well as those who trace their family roots to Kincardine. On behalf of everyone involved, thank you sincerely for your support – it is greatly appreciated.

Colin Anderson, April 2014

These for my friends in Tulliallan. In preparing these papers for publication I have the pleasant duty of thanking those who have been my helpers: the gentlemen of the Scottish Records Office (Historical Search Room) and of The National Library of Scotland, who brought me the documents and books I wished to consult, for their unfailing courtesy; the Librarian of The Edinburgh District Council for allowing me to read the minutes of the Dick Veterinary College; Dr John Wilson, Lochmaben, for the three illustrations to the paper on Sir James Wylie; the Trustees of The National Portrait Gallery and of The National Library of Scotland for permission to use the portrait of Sir James Dewar and those of Mr Robert and Sir Robert Maule; and Mr William Wolsey for providing me with a photograph of the premises of Robert Maule and Son. I am also to the rector and Archivist of Dollar Academy for their courteous reply to my queries.

To say "thank you" to Messrs How & Blackhall who have put their knowledge and skill as printers at my disposal, in this as in previous publications, is more than a polite gesture; it is an expression of genuine appreciation of the helpfulness and attention which have made it a pleasure to have been associated with them.

Of the inadequacy and imperfections of this necessarily brief account of these four eminent sons of Tulliallan I am well aware – and with the ancient writer would say, "If I have written well that is what I myself desired, but if poorly and indifferently this is all I could attain unto".

Rev. William Meiklejohn, M.A. January 1990.

6

Sir James Wylie

"There is but one way of explaining how great men appear at one time in the world and not at another and that is that God Almighty sometimes wills it and sometimes does not."

Autobiography of Sir Archibald Alison.

Figure 1: Portrait of Sir James Wylie

Figure 2: Sir James Wylie's Coat of Arms

Figure 3: The Sir James Wylie Memorial Hospital and the statue of Sir James

Biography

Towards the end of the year 1765 the marriage took place in Tulliallan Church, by the Rev. Robert Brown, of William Wylie, carrier in Kincardine and Janet Meiklejohn. Of that marriage there was a family of five sons. The eldest, William, became Master of the Public English School in Dundee (Note 1); the second, James, about whom we shall hear more presently, became a surgeon; the third son, George, followed his father's occupation; the fourth and the youngest, Robert and Walter respectively, became shipowners. The Wylies were in comfortable circumstances and were able to give two of their sons an education which fitted them for the teaching and medical professions. All five boys would attend the local

9

school which had been erected in 1694 on the North side of Tulliallan Church but much of their leisure time would be spent at the harbour, a busy and exciting place in those days, for, in the eighteenth century, Kincardine has a thriving seaport, outstripping Alloa in importance, having ninety locally registered vessels with a tonnage of over 5.461 tons. As many as nine ships were sometimes on the stocks, including sloops and brigantines, in addition to which there was a large number of fishing boats. What a playground that was for the alert, keen minded lads of the town! At the harbour they received a second education as they listened to sailors who had returned from lands afar, especially from the Baltic and the Low Countries, with which Kincardine had strong trading links, tell of their doings and seeings, of the towns and cities they had visited and of the peoples who inhabited them. To the Tulliallan boys, the names of the seaports of Holland and Belgium, of Germany, Denmark and Russia would be more familiar than those of their much nearer neighbour - England. Stories told at the quayside and recounted around the firesides on winter evenings, would stimulate the imagination of youth and kindle in the more venturesome a desire to see for themselves what they had heard described by their sailor friends.

On leaving school, James, whose ambition was to become a doctor, was apprenticed, as was customary in those days, to the local practitioner Dr. Meldrum, just as a lad today wishing to learn a trade is apprenticed to a plumber, a painter or a carpenter. James's apprenticeship did not run smoothly for "having been hardly dealt with" says his grandniece, "he ran off to sea". But he failed to reckon with his mother, "a woman of strong religious faith and character", who followed him to the small seaport of Cramond on the Forth and going on board a sloop lying there, dragged him ashore by the collar of his jacket and, it is said, "never relaxed her hold until she had him safe back in Kincardine". Darkness and a stormy night overtook them on the homeward journey and they were glad to seek shelter in a little cottage in a wood; a light from whose windows had guided them to the door. When the mother and son reached home she had walked more than forty miles in the accomplishment of her errand. "A sad pathetic interest," adds Miss Wylie, "attaches itself to the little sloop at Cramond, for, during the storm of the night she sank and when morning dawned nothing was seen of her but her mast above the water." So the mother that day saved not only her son's future career but probably his life also. The youthful runaway returned to his apprenticeship, for only by completing it successfully could he have gained entrance to Edinburgh University which he did in 1786, matriculating in that year and in the two succeeding years as a student of medicine, attending classes in anatomy, surgery, chemistry and in medical theory and practice in the first two of which he took a three-year course (Note 2). He was fortunate in his teachers, several of whom enjoyed an international reputation. In medicine and botany there was Daniel Rutherford who, in the year in which James commenced his studies, had succeeded Dr John Hope. The Professor of Anatomy was alexander Monro (secundus), a member of the Academies of Paris, Madrid, Berlin and Moscow and who, with his father and son, made quite outstanding contribution to the advancement of medical studies in Edinburgh. Dr Joseph Black, one of the most distinguished chemists Scotland has produced, occupied the Chair of Chemistry and the occupant of the Chair of the Practice of Medicine and Surgery was William Cullen who continued the method of clinical teaching which had been begun by Dr John Rutherford (Note 3). James Hamilton had been recently appointed the first Professor of Midwifery and John Thomson lectured on Pathology. During the latter part of the eighteenth century there was almost an obsession with founding societies of all kinds, at two of which - The Royal Medical Society and The Medico Chirurgical Society - students met in weekly session to submit and discuss papers on matters germane to their studies. It is not unlikely that young James Wylie participated in these and perhaps in other kindred societies as well. The Royal Infirmary, the predecessor of the present one adjacent to the Meadows which dates from 1870, had been opened in 1741 and was, by the standards of the eighteenth century, a spacious hospital with 228 beds and a large operating theatre. So, James Wylie received a thorough grounding in the various disciplines pertaining to medical and surgical treatment, which was to stand him in good stead in the land of his adoption. He left the University without graduating, which was a not uncommon custom in those days and which in no way reflects adversely on his ability or diligence. In 1790, at the age of twenty-two, he emigrated to Russia, becoming domiciled in St Petersburgh - now Leningrad - where he spent the remainder of his long life as a principal physician to three Czars, as their chief advisor on medical services in the army and as the founder, and for thirty years the Principal of the medical schools in Moscow and St Petersburgh, in all of which spheres he showed himself to be a man of five talents.

Why did he betake himself to Russia? A legend of doubtful veracity tells us that he had become involved in sheep stealing, which was in those days a very serious crime carrying with it severe penalties. To avoid this, we are told that he went into hiding and eventually escaped under a load of hay and then pushed off to sea (Note 4). No mention of such an escapade is made by his grandneice and like much local lore it should be viewed with caution. It is never easy to be sure of the motives, always mixed, which prompt us to take a particular course of action. It is much more difficult, if not impossible, to ascertain with certitude the motives of those who lived many years before us. Keeping this in mind it may, however, not be altogether inappropriate to suggest some of the factors which influenced young Dr Wylie in making up his mind to go to Russia. One, which has already been alluded to, may well have been a youthful desire for adventure and a wish to see for himself a country which had become familiar to him in boyhood as he had listened to the tales of sailor acquaintances, some of whom were lads of his own age. there was also the fact that although in industrial expertise and medical knowledge Russia lagged far behind the nations of Western Europe, she was now saying to them, like the Man of Macedonia, "Come over and help us". In the previous century Peter the Great had battered down the walls of partition which had separated Russia from her Western neighbours. During his reign, and largely due to his personal efforts, Russia emerged from her exclusiveness. In 1697 Peter paid a two-year visit to Europe. During his stay in Amsterdam he engaged personally in shipbuilding in the shipyards of Zaandam, acquiring all its skills, from naval architecture to ship carpentry, the latter of which he practised with his own hands. In England he found so much to engage his interest that he kept postponing the date of his departure. He also spent much time looking for suitable persons whom he could induce to come to Russia to instruct his people in the skills of their several trades, a line of action which met with marked success and which was continued, not, be it said, without considerable opposition in Britain, until long after his reign (Note 5). His two personal physicians were a German, Dr Blumenpost, and a Scotsman, Dr Robert Keith Erskine of Alva, the latter of whom accompanied the Emperor on his visit to the West (Note 6). In 1706 Peter had erected a military hospital in Moscow with a theatre and a school of surgery attached and in 1715 soldiers and sailors. What Peter had begun Catherine the Great, his successor, continued. She founded hospitals for the civilian sick, a medical college in St Petersburgh and encouraged foreign doctors to come, in even greater numbers, to settle in her Empire (Note 7). She was a caring ruler anxious to preserve the health of her people but her ambitions and plans far exceeded the available resources. By the end of the eighteenth century Russia had a considerable body of foreign medical practitioners, many of whom were Scotsmen, enjoying favourable conditions of employment with better prospects of advancement than in their native countries.

To a young surgeon like Wylie the opportunities to use his skill and so enlarge his practical experience by carrying out surgical operations, which only more experienced men at home would be allowed to undertake, would be an inducement to go abroad just as it is today to many graduates in medicine who emigrate for a few years to India, Africa and the Middle East and then return to occupy senior position in the medical services in Britain. Nor should we forget the unselfish idealism of youth which urges them to go to places where their skill in healing is so much more needed than in their own more adequately supplied homeland. The need is to the unselfish a call in itself.

Thus, impelled by a mixture of motives, all of them laudable, James Wylie sailed for Russia in 1790. So now it is over to Russia for us as it was then for him. Compared with Scotland, whose land mass is 30,000 square miles, Russia, stretching from China to the Baltic and from the Polar wastes of Siberia to the sub- tropical plains of the Crimea, is with its 8 3/4- million square miles, an exceedingly vast country. Its sheer bulk is staggering. At a time when the fastest speed of travel was that of the horse, it was an administrative nightmare. There were large 'no- go' areas where the implementation of enlightened legislation was well-nigh impossible and the lack of effective supervision allowed provincial rulers to indulge in corruption and perpetuate injustices unchecked and the landowners to treat their workers with cruel neglect and harshness. Beber, writing of the Emperor Alexander's concern for the peasants, records an occasion when he heard of a noble lady who lived at a considerable distance from Moscow and who habitually neglected her peasants as to sustenance and when they were ill. "He sent Dr Wiley, his own chief surgeon, to examine into the condition of the peasants with powers to act accordingly. After an inspection Dr Wiley sent for flour, meat and wine to the distance of 200 werts (Note 8) and obliged the offending lady to incur such heavy expenses that she was cured of ever again exercising so cruel and economy." One applauds the Emperor's action when such a case of "man's inhumanity to man" was brought to his notice - but how few were! It was not always want of will on the part of Russia's Czars that retarded improvements in social conditions but often the want of means to rectify such cruelties and injustices.

When young James Wylie came to Russia it was not only to a country sorely in need of medical aid but to a land in which there was already a sizeable colony of Scottish doctors, some of whom had won positions of eminence in their profession and in society and who, one is sure, would extend the hand of friendship to the new recruit. Among them was Dr Rogerson, a native of Dumfries, the doyen of the medical corps who had already given twenty-four years'service to medicine in Russia and who was highly esteemed in Court circles (Note 9). There was Robert Simpson who, having joined Admiral Greig's fleet in 1774, was now in 1790 chief surgeon to the naval hospital in Kronstadt. There was Charles Brown from Aberdeen who had come out in 1784; Alexander Crichton, head of the Civil Department of Medicine, and Dr Leighton, chief of the Naval Medical Services Department - and these are but a few. The Russians themselves were a warm-hearted and welcoming people. So the barometer of opportunity was set "fair" for the aspiring and enterprising young physician from Tulliallan.

Before proceeding to Russia he spent a brief period in Gothenburg in Sweden and then went to Riga where he found that, not having graduated at Edinburgh University, he had to undergo an examination at the medical college there, which he did successfully. Then, towards the end of the year, he entered upon what proved to be a long and illustrious period of service to Russia. His first assignment was to the Eletsky Regiment which he joined on Christmas Day 1790 and with which he was present at the siege of Warsaw in 1794 and of Cracow in 1795. His skill and diligence won the approbation of Colonel Fenshaw, a soldier of fortune, who in a society where educational facilities were sparse, was glad to engage Wylie as a tutor to one of his sons. So the young doctor's time was fully occupied not only with his responsibilities as a regimental surgeon, his study of the Russian language of which he gained a thorough mastery, his duties as the medical attendant to the family of Prince Galitzin, but also with his tutoring of Colonel Fenshaw's son, which would put a few extra roubles in his pocket. On 22nd December 1794 he was awarded the degree of MD by the University of Aberdeen. Dr Robert Lyall remarks that James Wylie "was reckoned a good surgeon and indeed was regarded as an expert and successful lithotomist and such was his skill that, young though he was, he was called upon to operate on several distinguished patients, one of whom was Baron Otto von Bloom, the Danish Ambassador, whose life he saved after taking over from Dr Rogerson and other senior surgeons who were baffled in their endeavours to effect a cure. It is not surprising, then, that in 1795 he was, on the recommendation of Dr Rogerson, appointed operator - or surgeon - to the Royal Household. His next step up the ladder of promotion had in it an element of luck - which comes to a man who makes his own luck. It happened that a nobleman, Count Kutaisof, a dear and valued friend of the Czar, Paul 1, was suffering from a throat complaint; and, as Wylie's grandniece recounts the incident,

17

"the seriousness of the case being discussed in the hospital where Dr Wylie was, he made the remark that he thought that if he saw the Count he could do something for him. This saying was reported in the patient's home but the doctors in attendance were very jealous of another's skill superseding their own, and it was only when they regarded the case as utterly hopeless that young Wylie was sent for. He obeyed the summons and on entering the sick room performed what is now well known as the simple operation of tracheotomy, but which at that time was totally unknown in Russia." The patient soon breathed freely. The operation proved a complete success. Intelligence of this was communicated immediately to the Emperor who had been waiting to hear of his friend's demise. Next day the Czar sent for the young doctor and before the interview ended Wylie was placed on the Czar's personal staff and assigned rooms in the Royal Palace. Miss Wylie adds: "In connection with the operation case, the wildest and most vague stories were put in circulation and by many people actually believed in! There was nothing however sensational about it. It was simply what I have stated." The happy outcome was due entirely to Dr Wylie's superior knowledge and to the advanced technique which he had acquired in Edinburgh. For many years afterward the witty comment was often made by his friends, that Wylie owed his promotion to cutting Count Kutaisof's throat - a joke which the subject of it, who often recounted it himself, enjoyed as much as anyone. This operation was not alone in advancing James Wylie's already considerable reputation. "Some other cases soon afterwards occurred where his knowledge and skill triumphed over the ignorance of his contemporaries", Dr Lyall tells us; adding not only to the general esteem in which

Wylie was held but engendering also considerable professional jealousy which made him "the subject of numerous plans to accomplish his ruin but he defeated them all by his extreme watchfulness, assiduity and interest".

What truth there may be - or not be - in another tale which gained credence and wide circulation, the reader must judge for himself. The story goes that the Emperor Paul, who was mentally unstable, complained of buzzings in his ear. Wylie, who realised that this was due to psychological rather than to physical causes, was said to have introduced by skilful sleight of hand, a bee into the Czar's ear which he subsequently extracted, showed the Czar and from that moment the sufferer was freed from his annoyance. Mss Wylie does not mention this incident. But if it is authentic it is a tribute to the young doctor's shrewd understanding of his patient rather than to his medical expertise. As physician to the Emperor he was in attendance on him on his journeys to Moscow and on his visits to more distant parts of the empire such as Kazan. But his association with Paul 1 was short-lived. As the years passed the Czar's mental condition deteriorated. Always unbalanced and moody he was inclined to by tyrannical. Now he became sadistic and so far had he fallen below the level of sanity that by 1799 even his son Alexander, a humane mild mannered man, realised that steps had to be taken to remove his father from the throne (Note 10). His wish was that Paul should have abdicated and gone into luxurious retirement but there was no prospect of the Emperor agreeing to such a desirable event. the denouement came on the night of 11th March 1801 when a group of officers whom he had deeply offended became a bunch of drunken conspirators who burst into the Czar's bedroom and despite his shrill cries for help and immense personal strength, strangled him with a long scarf. Though they had armed themselves with knives, one of the British doctors, Grieve by name, who attended the embalming of the body which was carried out by Dr Wylie, said that he observed no cuttings consistent with the use of sharp knives but that there was evidence of a broad contused area round the neck which indicated strangulation. News of the Czar's death was received everywhere, and not least in the Army, with relief. The official death certificate, signed by James Wylie, declared that Paul 1 had died of apoplexy, a fiction which, for political reasons, was deemed prudent and which, we are told, "gave the Court great satisfaction". Whatever suspicions there may have been regarding its truth, this misinformation was maintained in print for a hundred years. Though by 1844 the writer of "Letters from the Baltic" could say that the death by strangulation of Paul 1 "is a subject now discussed without any great reserve" and she even named the individual who was credited with the deed - Count Pahlen (Note 11). It was not, however, until 1907 that in a biography by Shumigorsky the true story of Paul's demise was given to the world. Rigid censorship had seen to its suppression. Thus in March 1801 the four years reign of what is known in Russian history as "the rule of the madman" came to an end.

His son and successor, Alexander I, under whom Dr Wylie was to serve for the next twenty-four years, had been cast in a very different mould. He was a man with whom the Scottish doctor had the closest rapport. If, by the death of Paul I Russia had lost a despotic tyrant she found in his successor a benevolent ruler. All who have written about him eulogise his humanity, his passion for justice, his keen interest in education, the arts and hospitals, the last of which he was most assiduous in visiting in every part of his wide domains to which he travelled. Writing in 1825 Dr Robert Lyall says, "I shall never forget the first time I saw His Majesty, a few days after his return from Paris in 1815. I was introduced to Sir James Wylie with whom I visited some of the military hospitals in St Peterburg and in which I spoke with a number of medical gentlemen. A few days afterwards, on the Palace Quay, at no great distance from one of these hospitals, I remarked an officer in plain uniform without epaulettes, whom I took to be one of the physicians I had seen and meant to address him. But for my want of knowledge of the French language at that time I should have addressed him. While I hesitated to say - "Comment vous portez vous, Monsieur le Docteur" or simply "Docteur" the Emperor came upon me, stared and passed by. But what was my astonishment at seeing a number of persons one after the other standing to one side and taking off their hats as the said officer proceeded forward. On enquiry, I found that I had taken the Emperor for a doctor!" When, in 1818, Alexander I entertained the King of Prussia, one of the scheduled visits was to an hospital. Quoting Dr Lyall again there is this: "On his arrival at a town, as soon as time permits, Alexander visits and examines the state of the public institutions and the hospitals, especially the military hospitals, with the minutest attention. Indeed, so quick is His Majesty in his motions to these places that he sometimes arrives unexpectedly at an earlier hour than looked for and finds the establishment in its real state. As I have heard Sir James Wylie, who is not slow in his duty, state that it had oftener happened than once that the Emperor had visited the military hospitals before he had done so himself, through as Head of Medical Staff of the Army they fall peculiarly under his care and direction." That the Emperor should take so personal an interest in military hospitals is not surprising when we remember how vulnerable Russia was to invasion from the West, as was demonstrated in 1812 by Napoleon's march on Moscow.

As the Navy was our nation's strong shield in the nineteenth century, so the Army was Russia's strong wall of defence. Thus as administrative head of the Military Medical Services, James Wylie was fortunate in having the enthusiastic support of the Emperor in the wide-ranging reforms in the Military Hospitals which he was to initiate and carry through.

As a regimental surgeon James Wylie was well aware of how inadequate was the provision made for the medical care of the wounded. One doctor, without any semi-skilled auxiliaries to aid him, was allocated to 1600 men. On the field of battle no provision was made to carry the wounded to first-aid posts - which anyway were non-existent! and when darkness fell and the fighting ceased hundreds of wounded men were abandoned to perish where they lay. A not inhumane officer remarked that "a cannon ball was the best friend for a man who had lost a limb"; a quick death being preferable to a long dark night of agony before the inevitable happened. That, in the space of a few years, things were very different, is due to the efforts and organising skill of James Wylie. In the British and Foreign Medical Journal for 1836, Dr George Lefevre, physician to the British Embassy in Russia, writes: "The common soldier has to thank Sir James Wylie for such care and protection as his predecessors demanded in vain; and the army in general has to thank him for a real and effective, instead of a nominal an inefficient, medical staff. It is not necessary," he concludes, "to refer to very remote periods to show by comparison how much he has done for the wounded soldier." As a regimental surgeon Dr Wylie had been present at the Battle of Austerlitz in December 1805 when, in killed and wounded, Russia and her allies had lost more than thirty-thousand men, and again at the Battle of Jena in 1806 when there was a considerable carnage and he must have seen how inadequate, to the point of non-existence, were the facilities for treating the wounded. By the following year there was some improvement. After the Battle of Eylau, in February 1807, there were hospitals available at Konigsberg: and when, after sever losses, the Russians and their allies fell back on that town, several thousands had their wounds dressed regularly. But still, the number who perished by lingering deaths on the battlefield was far greater. By June of that year there was further improvement in organisation and at the Battle of Friedland on 14th June the wounded were attended on the field of battle for the first time. "To James Wylie," says General Wilson, "goes the merit for this improvement that the wounded were dressed under the fire of cannon." No one was more active in caring for the wounded than Wylie himself and while he took a full share in treating the wounded at the many battles - some twenty in all - at which he was present, his herculean achievement was at the Battle of Borodino in September 1812, one of the bloodiest battles of the Napoleonic Wars, in which both sides exhausted themselves, and the Russians lost forty-five thousand men, and where he

23

personally attended to two hundred wounded soldiers on the field (Note 12). On the following night he rode with the Cossacks, under the command of Platoff, deep into the French lines (Note 13). In these wars he was wounded three times and on his own reckoning he travelled with the army, on foot or on horseback, in a carriage or on a sledge, more than 150,000 miles. His devotion and outstanding service to the wounded at the Battle of Borodino was long remembered. In 1840, on the anniversary of the Battle of Borodino, a medal was struck by the Emperor Nicholas bearing on one side a profile of Sir James Wylie. From the site of the battle, where celebrations were being held, the Emperor wrote to Sir James, now in his seventy- third year. "I cannot but call to mind the services which you rendered on that memorable epoch when, at the head of the Corps of medical and surgical officers of the Army, you yourself ceased not to give a grand example of zeal and self-denial for the welfare and relief of the suffering warriors." The heroism of the Russian soldier in battle is proverbial but no less courageous was he when wounded and undergoing surgery, always in these days without an anaesthetic. General Wilson recalls an incident of just such remarkable bravery which he himself witnessed. "I saw a Cossack having his arm extracted at the shoulder joint after having ridden twenty miles from where he had been struck by a cannon ball. He never spoke during the operation which was performed by Dr Wylie in less than four minutes but afterwards he talked quite composedly. Next morning he drank tea, walked about the room and then got into a cart for a fourteen-mile journey home. According to reports he made a good recovery." The operation of extracting an injured arm was a quite frequent one and seldom failed to cure. No less courageous was General Moreau at the time of the Battle of Leipzig. As he was in conversation with the Emperor and Lord Cathcart, the British Ambassador (Note 14), Moreau was struck by a cannon ball. Let General Wilson, who was in their company, relate what happened: "Moreau, who was on horseback, suddenly cried 'oh!' and threw himself from his horse with one leg shattered and the inside of his other knee mangled. The horse, through whose body the cannon ball had passed, staggered and fell down beside his master. Moreau exclaimed: 'C'est passe avec moi! Mon affaire est faite", as he looked at his legs. On the Emperor's instructions, some Cossacks lifted him on their pikes and carried him to the nearest village where Wylie was tending the wounded. The surgeon promptly amputated both legs." Moreau bore it like a soldier without a word and during the whole day kept a cheerful serenity which proved the possession of extraordinary powers of mind, when one remembers that the operation was performed without an anaesthetic. During the next few days, as the army moved on, he was carried by thirty soldiers, detailed for the duty, as the roads were quite unfit for a carriage. He succumbed six days later and was buried in St Petersburgh. On one occasion General Wilson himself became the patient. Returning home about midnight he had a nasty spill when the droska (Note 15) in which he was travelling overturned and he was thrown heavily on to the road. His legs and ankles were severely injured. Dr Wylie dressed the deep cuts and ordered the patient to stay in bed. But the General, who had important duties requiring attention, went out next day and when the doctor saw him later and how swollen his ankles had become and how angry was the wound, he gave the General such a dressing down that - to quote his own words - "I remained indoors and wrote despatches until he gave me permission to go out." Accidents and illness are no respecters of persons. Doctors are not immune from either. In 1824 Dr Wylie had a serious accident with his carriage. This gave the Emperor Alexander, whom he had served for more than twenty years, a chance to show his appreciation of his services. The Emperor remained with him for three days and sat at his bedside for hours. On leaving, he gave orders that every comfort should be provided for the patient and that couriers should be sent daily to him with reports of Dr Wylie's progress until the patient was completely out of danger.

Miss Wylie has this to say about the condition of the military hospitals when her grand-uncle arrived in Russia in 1790. "The buildings were in a deplorable state. The laws of health in regard to light and ventilation were totally disregarded. It was difficult to convince the people that the buildings were at fault and to demonstrate his theory he used the simple means of placing plants in the various windows. Those exposed to the south flowered; the others either remained green or withered. Once the idea was caught, they were ready to pull down the hospitals and rebuild them according to his - Dr Wylie's - plans." Such, then, was the unsatisfactory position regarding hospital accommodation in the pre-Wylie era. Now let us hear the verdict of a doctor who, in the post-Wylie era, visited the Military Hospital in Moscow, situated in a high and airy suburb, with an elegant frontage and two extensive wings. "When I last visited this hospital in January 1819, it contained twelve-hundred patients but is capable of receiving fifteen-hundred. Opposite the foreign burying ground are a number of one-storey, wooden, yellow painted houses, which belong also to this hospital and which are provided with beds for three-hundred-and-fifty sick. At this establishment everything seems conveniently arranged. There is a receiving room where the patients are examined by a physician or surgeon and accepted: a bathroom and baths well supplied with cold and warm water in which those admitted, when their state allows of it, are all well bathed and cleaned, or in which the sick receive particular baths by order of the physician and a room for the deposition of the patients' own clothes when they receive the dress of the hospital. Upstairs, in the centre of the front, a grand saloon with a lofty arched roof, embellished in the ends by Corinthian pillars, contains pictures of Peter the Great, Catherine I, Elizabeth and Catherine II. From this hall is the entry into the balcony opposite to the summer gardens from which the view is extensive and pleasant. This hall is destined for the reception of the Emperor who never fails to visit this hospital when he comes to Moscow.

Most of the wards are immensely large and capable of containing a hundred-and-twenty beds. A single ward occupies the whole breadth of the building. In the centre, running lengthwise a partial division is formed by broad based pillars between which are arched communications. Ranges of beds are disposed along the walls of these wards and along each side of the pillars. The bedsteads are of wood painted green. Each patient has two sheets, the upper one of which is stitched as usual to the counterpane. There is a small table between every two beds on which stand pewter dishes for each patient, his medicines, etc. The clothes of the sick are good. The heating of the wards in winter and the ventilation at all times are excellently managed. The floor of the hospital is painted of a brownish yellow colour and is kept clean. Indeed we found everything in the cleanest and best order. The eye is delighted with the view of these immense wards and the heart charmed with their utility. The Military Hospital is a splendid establishment. It does the highest honour to the empire and to all those concerned in its direction. The cost per patient is little more than half that of Civil Hospitals - 10 to 12 kopecks per day." What is true of this hospital would be equally true of all the others for which Dr Wylie had responsibility, and no finer tribute to the excellence of his achievement can be paid than the appreciation by the eminent doctor which has just been quoted.

During the early years of the nineteenth century Europe was in turmoil. The armies of Napoleon had been rampaging across the continent beating into subjection one nation after another. Between him and complete domination of Europe there stood a small island - Great Britain - with her omnipotent navy, which she employed, not only to keep her own shores inviolate, but to halt and search the merchant vessels of neutral nations, in order to ensure that they were not carrying supplies to the enemy. This unilateral action was an irritant which the neutral countries resented. Among them was Russia, whose mad ruler, Paul I, favoured Napoleon. He banned British ships from the Baltic and several, which risked running the gauntlet of his navy, were captured. Among the unfortunates was the Ann Spittal of Kincardine whose captain, Robert Spittal, and crew, were interned. One of them, John Wilcox, was a Stirlingshire man whose mother lived at St Ninians. Realising the discomforts her son would be experiencing and eager for his release, she ventured on a droll plan which united faith and works. She set off to Paisley, where the finest silk in Scotland was manufactured; walking all the way and back, some sixty miles. There she selected the best silk thread available, with which she knitted a pair of socks, in the Troy pattern which was very fashionable in Scotland at the time. Illiterate herself, she secured the good offices of the local schoolmaster to pen a letter to the Czar of Russia appealing for clemency for her boy. Enclosing with it the socks which she had knitted as a gift to the Emperor; and knowing that Kincardine ships sailed to the Baltic, she found a sea captain who agreed to act as an intermediary and convey the parcel to James Wylie who, she rightly jaloused, would deliver it personally to the Czar. Such was Wylie's influence that her son, John, soon appeared at his mother's cottage door in St Ninians and such was Dr Wylie's generosity, that John had with him a substantial sum of money for his mother. Anxious to have some tangible memento of the success of her ploy, Betty Willox went to the local clockmaker whom she requested to make a grandfather clock, on which was inscribed the homespun rhyme: "Wha'd hae thoucht it Stockings bocht it" and for many years afterward that pleasing piece of furniture graced Betty Willox's humble cottage. (Note 16)

If, initially, under Paul I Russia's sympathies had been with the French, Alexander, his successor, came quickly to realise that the true interests of his people lay with the Allied Nations whose side he eventually supported. As with Hitler, any treaty which Napoleon signed became "a scrap of paper" as soon as its terms conflicted with his long-term ambition to conquer

Europe (Note 17). In 1812 Napoleon's armies moved northwards, bent on the subjugation of Russia. The story of their eventual frustration is familiar - how, after being worsted in the bloody battle of Borodino, the Russians retreated in order, luring Napoleon on towards Moscow, and then, with sacrificial courage, set fire to their capital in order to deny the invading army any vestige of food or shelter; and then, how, amid unspeakable sufferings, the French had to retreat, harassed all the way along by the wild Russian Cossacks under their indomitable leader Platoff and battered by "General Winter" who devoured more than were slain by the sword.

Early in his career, Wylie realised that importing doctors from the West was only tinkering with Russia's problem. Nothing short of an indigenous medical profession, trained to the same high standards as Scottish doctors, was needed and that could be achieved only by the establishment of a medical college. It was a daunting enterprise but, with the active encouragement of the Emperor Alexander, Dr Wylie put his hand to the plough and never looked back until his dream was realised. Four years before he had set foot in Russia, Catherine the Great had, with a gift of a hundred-and-twenty-five-thousand roubles, established a Medical Academy in Moscow, which fell prey to the flames in 1812, when the city was reduced to ashes. That gave Wylie his opportunity. A large three-storied building with doric pillars, formerly a wealthy man's residence, became available. The Government purchased it and it became the nucleus of the new training college for doctors. Large extensions were added to it and inscribed on the pediment was the cipher of Alexander I with, in Russian,

30

the inscription - "The Medico-Chirugical Academy". A similar building was erected in St Petersburgh and, for thirty years, Sir James Wylie was the head of both, each of which was superintended by a vice-president. Both institutions were modelled on what he himself had known as a student in Edinburgh University, with such modifications as experience in Russia had shown him to be advisable. Each Academy was equipped with an anatomical museum and a botanical garden. There were three departments of study - a Medical Section, a Veterinary Section and a Pharmaceutical Section; to which was added instruction in Latin, Greek and German, three languages useful to every medical student - the first two as an aid to medical nomenclature and the third, a language in which many current treatises were written. The annual cost of the maintenance of the St Petersburgh college was one-hundred-and- sixty-nine thousand three-hundred roubles and of the Moscow College one-hundred-and-forty-seven thousand three-hundred- and-forty roubles, to which was added sixty-nine thousand six- hundred-and-fifty roubles, being expenses common to both, including the cost of pensions for professors, prizes to the best students, uniform for the pupils on their discharge, travelling expenses and the upkeep of the libraries and museums. To have inspired and carried through two such schemes was no mean achievement and to have presided over them successfully for thirty years constitutes no small contribution to the medical history of the land of his adoption. In the words of The British and Foreign Medical Journal of April 1836, "It is to Sir James Wylie that Russia is indebted for the organisation of her medical schools both civil and military and it has been by his persevering industry that the Medical Academy of Petersburgh and

Moscow has arrived at the honourable rank which it now holds among medical institutions."

We turn once more to the international scene. The Battle of Dresden in August 1813 was the last of Napoleon's great victories. Thanks to Wellington's successful campaign in the Iberian Peninsula and to the victory of the Allies at Leipzig, that evil man was gradually pushed into a corner like a rat and no one was more determined on his destruction than Alexander, the Emperor of Russia. On 31st March 1814 the Allies, with Alexander at their head, entered Paris where their coming was welcomed by the populace as a great deliverance from evil. The warmth of feeling, shown in the reception accorded to Wellington and to the other Allied leaders, outdid anything demanded by mere courtesy. Among those attending the Paris Peace Conference was a large Russian delegation led by their Emperor who, with his personal physician, Dr Wylie, took up residence in the finest hotel in the city. With the outbreak of peace the continent was once more open to British tourists and among those who visited Paris were four young Scots: Archibald Alison, his brother and two friends (Note 18). Armed with letters of introduction to the British Ambassador, Lord Cathcart, whose Scottish home was at Shawpark, Alloa, and to Dr Wylie whose family lived in Kincardine, the four Scots lads met several Russian army officers and even the Emperor "whose dignified and courteous manners and simple character" impressed them greatly. Dr Wylie, who had no responsibilities so far as the Peace Conference went, put himself out to entertain them. To show their appreciation of the kindness they had received, the four youths entertained sixteen Russians and Britons to dinner at the Restaurant Malpinot in the Rue Saint Honore, and the fact that in his autobiography, written many years later, Alison says that among the guests "was James Wylie" is clear evidence of the place which the Tulliallan doctor had won in their regard. Being so near to England it was natural that the Emperor should pay a visit to the land of his principal ally. He took with him Count Tolstoy, Platoff the intrepid Cossack leader, and Dr Wylie. Having negotiated The Peace of Paris, which treaty he signed on 30th May, he left the French capital on 2nd June and landed at Dover at 6.30a.m. on the 6th of June. In reply to the Mayor's Address of Welcome, Alexander spoke "of his long standing desire to see England, a country for which I have the highest esteem". Though luxurious accommodation had been prepared for him in London at Cumberland House, he chose to reside at Pultney's Hotel, where his sister was staying (Note 19) and from where he sallied forth, accompanied no doubt by Wylie, to visit hospitals and kindred institutions. While they were attending the Ascot Races, the Emperor requested the Regent - later King George IV - to confer the Order of Knighthood on Dr Wylie, and taking Platoff's sword, for no English one was at hand, the Regent gladly complied. A few days later, Sir James, as we must now call him, was accorded the higher dignity of a Baronetcy of the The United Kingdom. He does not appear to have visited his native Scotland on this occasion as one might have expected, but he invited his brother, William, to go to London with his family and when they were there he gave them some valuable presents and on his departure gave £500 for his five nieces. After his return to Russia he sent further gifts to William and his family among which were his portrait, two valuable gold cases and a gold

33

inlaid fowling piece. Among the Wylie family whom he entertained in London was William's son, Dr John Wylie, minister of Carluke whom he asked to become his private secretary. The request was declined. When, in 1847, The Rev. Dr Wylie was on a visit to St Petersburgh, he received from his uncle various valuable presents as tokens of regard. A happy meeting took place in Rotterdam in 1814 when Walter was at Rotterdam with his ship and Sir James arrived there in the entourage of the Emperor Alexander. On that occasion Sir James gave his brother "a chronometer watch". Almost every year afterwards, for some time, Walter had occasion to be in St Petersburgh with his vessel and invariably the brothers "visited and dined with each other, the physician often sending presents to his other relatives in Kincardine and in 1826 he gave Walter £500". Sir James, we are told, "seems to have been averse to letter writing and communicated with his friends verbally or by means of messages conveyed by persons passing to and fro". But when opportunity offered he was most generous to his relatives.

Nothing is more astounding than the recuperative power of Napoleon. When the nations of Europe reckoned that, having been banished to Elba, he would trouble them no more, that evil man reappeared on the continent. Having raised an army, he began to wage war afresh and ceased only when he was decisively beaten by Wellington at Waterloo and subsequently banished to St Helena. Under the strain of the war, during which his country had been invaded and his capital burnt to ashes; and then finding that the Congress of Vienna was making scant progress towards the establishment of an enduring peace, the Emperor's health, physical and mental, began to bend. Sir James Wylie had a very anxious time as Alexander became increasingly neurotic, a prey to phobias and to the fear of assassination by dissident groups. He who had loved to move freely among his people, now refused to venture out unless his guards first searched both sides of the street. While on holiday at Czarco-Selo, the Emperor was caught in a prolonged and violent shower of sleet which brought on a severe chill. That night he refused dinner. In the early morning he was attacked by fever and erysipalis which, first appearing on his leg quickly affected the rest of his body. He began to suffer from bouts of delirium and, in a covered sledge he was taken to St Petersburgh for the attention of the best medical advisers in the country. Their unanimous opinion was that, as signs of gangrene were apparent, the offending leg should be amputated. Sir James alone disagreed and with Scottish cuteness, he warned them that if the Emperor, who was not in the best of health, succumbed during the operation they would be blamed, whereas if he died from the disease they would be held blameless. Confident in the rightness of his opinion, and never was his clinical judgment more shrewd, he took full responsibility for the patient. Gradually the disease yielded to cautery and the lancet and eventually the healing process was complete. On Wylie's advice the Emperor was now restricted to a vegetarian and fruit diet, to prevent a recurrence of the trouble. But, though he resumed his duties and continued to travel long distances throughout his vast domains, where he was everywhere received with rapturous welcomes, nothing was able to rouse him from melancholia.

In November 1825 Alexander visited the Crimea travelling nine- hundred miles in seventeen days. Halting at Yoursouf he dined, very frugally, with Count Voronzov the Governor. There were oysters at dinner and a small worm was seen adhering to the shell of one presented to the Emperor. It was shown to Sir James who pronounced it harmless. This led on to talking about insects and the Emperor enquired if there were any scorpions in the Crimea, which prompted Sir James to remind him of the scorpion which was found in his bed at Verona and of the prescription Sir James had written for the cure of the bite. After some general conversation about homeopathy, in which the emperor had recently taken an interest, he thanked his host for his entertainment and his fellow guests for the satisfaction their company had given him. Next day the party left for Sevastopol. During the journey the Emperor became unnaturally cold and was subject to bouts of shivering. The inn, at which they put up overnight, left much to be desired and, before retiring, Sir James gave the Emperor a glass of hot punch which seemed to revive him. Next day they reached Taganrog and though he seemed worse, Alexander was confident that his strong constitution allied to the medication Sir James had prescribed, would see him through. The only three things he sought were sleep, quiet and cold water, of which his doctor vetoed the last. A few days later the Emperor became decidedly worse. At times he was delirious, talking of the awful carnage of the battles he had witnessed, of the burning of Moscow, and of the assassination of his father, Paul I. Fixing his eyes on Wylie, he said, "It was a horrible act. He was not even permitted to say the prayer that a dying man owes to his Maker". Though Sir James and Dr Stoffrogen, who had been called in for consultation, decided that the patient should be bled, the Emperor resolutely refused. He seemed almost to have formed a death wish. A few days later his condition was such that Sir James informed the Empress that her husband was dying and when, at her request, the doctor informed the patient himself, Alexander replied: "Then you think that I am dying", and as he pressed Sir James's hand he added, "that is the best news I have heard in years." As he slipped in and out of delirium he said to Sir James, "Ah! my friend, I think you are deceived as to the nature of my illness - it is my nerves that need a cure." On the morning of the 30th November when the curtains were drawn back and the sunlight streamed into the room, he exclaimed, "Ah! le beau jour!" These were the Emperor's last conscious words. Next day in the presence of Sir James Wylie, his good physician, the Empress and two others, the Emperor Alexander died - and Russia lost one of her most beneficent rulers (Note 11). For Wylie it had been a harrowing time. Alexander was not only his Emperor whom he had served for almost a quarter of a century but a close and valued friend for whom he had deep affection.

After the Emperor's death Dr Robert Lee was sent by Count Voronzov, Governor of the Crimea, to ascertain officially the nature of the Emperor's illness. Let us hear in his own account. "Sir James Wylie read to me the whole of the reports of His Majesty's case, written down by him from day to day and which contained the fullest and most satisfactory explanation of all the attendant circumstances. These reports were also signed by the other physicians called in, who coincided in the views entertained by Sir James respecting the nature and proposed treatment of the disease." During the interview Dr Reinhold, the surgeon to the Empress, came in and "declared to me that he was entirely of the same opinion." The hardest blow of all to Sir James must have been his knowledge that the Emperor's ailment - Crimean Fever - was curable, if the patient had accepted the advice which Wylie had tendered. All along, the Emperor had declared adamantly that he would recover without surgical treatment and "though both doctors insisted in a most decided way," says Lee, "that he should be bled and that certain drugs should be administered, the Emperor would not listen - even though the Empress herself pleaded with him." A post mortem examination revealed that Sir James' diagnosis had been correct and when some doctors said they would have forced the Emperor to have undergone the treatment, Sir James replied that he was not prepared to commit the crime of lese majeste which, in his view, no circumstances could justify. Dr Lee concludes his official report with these words, "I enjoyed the best opportunities in the Crimea of observing the devoted attachment of Sir James Wylie to the Emperor Alexander, whom he had accompanied in all his campaigns, and I conscientiously believe that on this trying occasion Sir James discharged his arduous professional duty in a manner worthy of his high reputation."

The new Emperor, Nicolas - and this is a tribute to both the personal esteem in which Dr Wylie was held and to the confidence of The Court in his professional competence - continued Sir James's appointment as the Czar's personal physician. Nicolas was a robust, healthy, military man who probably required little medical attention. Scant mention is made of Sir James Wylie's activities during his reign, though

Dr Lee does provide one interesting sidelight: In 1826, relations between Russia and Turkey had become strained and in April war was thought to be imminent. On 1st May Admiral Greig and Sir James Wylie received orders to hold themselves in readiness. Then, when Lee happened to be with Sir James, news came that the Turks had acceded to Russia's demands and that the expected war was off. "I saw manifest disappointment on the visage of Sir James Wylie," comments Dr Lee. By 1826 the period of constructive innovation was over. The Army Medical Service had been placed on a firm foundation. The military hospitals had been brought up to date. The two Medical Colleges in Moscow and St Petersburgh had been founded, equipped and a comprehensive curriculum of instruction devised. The role of Sir James was now changed from that of innovator to the no less essential one of administrator. He was regarded by all who were in a position to know as a first- class administrator. His remaining years of service, if outwardly less spectacular, were as active and as useful in the cause of medicine in Russia as had been his former years.

When James Wylie came to Russia in 1790 the library of medical textbooks was extremely meagre - some say there were only three available in the Russian language. He made a significant contribution towards rectifying this sorry state of affairs. In 1805 the Emperor commissioned him "to consider preventative and curative instructions for the Russian troops" who were stationed in Corfu and other Greek islands and who were threatened with a deadly disease known variously as The Yellow Fever or The American Plague. The outcome of his investigation was contained in a book, printed by The Russian

Medical Press and dedicated to the Czar, which gave a fairly exhaustive treatment of the subject with an historical account of its origin, a consideration of its causes and recommendations for its cure. Twenty years later, it was followed by another study of the disease entitled Practical Remarks on the Plague. At the same time he prepared a Russian translation of James Johnson's classic study on "The Influence of Tropical Climate on European Constitutions". One of his earliest publications was "A Handbook on Surgical Operations". It was published in 1806 and was the first book of its kind in Russian. It proved immensely useful to both doctors and students, coming as it did from a man, young though he was, who was an acknowledged authority on surgery and who possessed also the gift of lucid exposition. His magnum opus was The Pharmocopoeia Castrenis Ruthiena which appeared in 1808 and which was so comprehensive and authoritative that it went through several editions and remained the standard text book on the subject for more than half a century.

Miss Wylie, his grandniece, writes: "His tastes and habits of life were very simply. Although possessed of a splendid residence he usually sat in a small room containing only a writing table and two chairs and half a dozen favourite dogs lying on the floor." When at home, he, soldier-like, made his midday repast on black bread and salt but he frequently, according to the custom of the country, went to some acquaintance, either in the palace or the city, where he dined as a member of the family. So far as is known, he never visited Tulliallan though we know of his having been seised in a tenement of houses in Kincardine in April 1823 belonging to the sequestrated estate of George Millar, shipmaster, to whom he had given two loans of £150 each. If he never returned to his native heath, several of his relatives visited him in Russia. His mother, wishing to judge for herself of her son's success, went out to visit him, though he tried to persuade her not to do so. But she was determined and went. After a short stay she returned to Kincardine, possessed of many gifts, including some very fine silken shawls and an exquisite china tea set which the Czar had presented to her.

"His youngest brother, Walter, visited him several times when his ship, named The Baronet, went to St Peterburgh. On one occasion, Walter was presented to the Emperor and was invited by His Majesty to dine with him that evening. There were present the Emperor himself, three of his nobles, Sir James and my grandfather. The service was of gold plate. French was the language usually spoken at the Royal Table and at Court, but, in consideration of the Scotchman's nationality, the conversation was carried on in English, an act of courtesy my grandfather never forgot." Walter received many gifts from his brother, among them being a beautiful gold and platinum cup and saucer and two large and costly diamond rings. "My father, William Wylie," his daughter tells us, "when a sailor boy, saw him in St Petersburgh and received from him a large silver pen and pen holder which combined with a mathematical instrument. Other relatives also received generous gifts. Two of his eldest brothers' sons went out from Dundee to their uncle and prospered greatly. A grandnephew Mr Richard Wylie, a son of Dr John Wylie, minister of Carluke and grandson of William Wylie, Master of the English School in Dundee, was for many years one of the

41

most respected citizens of St Petersburgh. David Wylie, a son of Sir James's brother Robert, died in Moscow in 1836. In June 1829 he was visited by a niece who had married Mr Alexander Edward, a Dundee merchant and to both of them Sir James showed much kindness and spoke with great affection about his relatives in Scotland. To Mrs Edward he gave a costly diamond ring which he had received from the late Queen of Russia and to Mr Edward a Siberian topaz and a seal which had been gifts to him from the Emperor Alexander. Afterwards, on different occasions, he sent to Mrs Edward a very fine Persian cloak, a pocket Bible which his mother had given to him, his portrait and a medal which had been struck on the occasion of celebrations in St Petersburgh to mark the fiftieth anniversary of his service under the Russian Government. During their visit to Russia Sir James spoke to Mr and Mrs Edward of his intention to purchase an estate in Scotland and requested Mr Edward to look out for a suitable property. He had no desire to leave Russia and return permanently to Scotland but he wished to have a home in his native land where he could enjoy "a month or two of sport in an interesting district". He was interested in acquiring Havieston Estate, near Dollar, and also entered into negotiations for the purchase of Glen Ogil Estate near Kirriemuir but he said he had no wish to possess "a large mansion knowing from experience that such is the cause of considerable annoyance and anxiety". With a view to making available in Scotland funds for the purchase of an estate, Sir James placed £50,000 in British Bonds at 3% so that the money would be immediately forthcoming.

Sir James Wylie, who was unmarried, died in St Petersburg on 2nd March 1854. His funeral was attended by the Czar and all the Court notables. Besides having had a Baronetcy of The United Kingdom conferred upon him he had been the recipient of many honours from Russia and other countries and among the gifts received from the Imperial Family was a large silver watch suitably inscribed. By his Will he made financial provision for an appropriate funeral and for the erection of a monument at his grave. Having no direct heirs he bequeathed his very considerable fortune to the Emperor Nicolas and the Russian nation for the construction of "a large hospital at St Petersurgh to be attended by the pupils of the Medico-Chirugical Academy" where they could receive clinical instruction. On Christmas Day 1869, the anniversary of the day in 1790 when he had entered the service of Russia as surgeon to the Eletsky Regiment, a handsome memorial in the courtyard of The Wylie Clinical Hospital was dedicated to his memory (Note 20). It represents Dr Wylie seated on a rock, attired in the parade uniform of a military surgeon. At his feet lies his book on "Military Pharmacy"; his left hand, holding a paper scroll and his right grasping a pencil shows him in the attitude of penning his thoughts on the organisation of military institutions in Russia. The statue is of bronze and the pedestal on which it stands is of Finland black marble. It is adorned by caryatides emblematic of Hygeia, the Greek goddess of health. On the four sides of the pedestal are the doctor's coat of arms in bronze, a representation of the first meeting of the Academy, a picture in bronze of his activity on the battlefield in 1813, 1814 and 1815, and the dedicatory inscription. His coat of arms consists of a shield divided horizontally into two parts, the upper portion showing the

43

Imperial Coat of Arms of Russia, beneath which is a silver sword and on the lower portion there is an open hand and two five-pointed stars. The Shield is surmounted by an open helmet and a Cossack of the Don in the act of jumping from his horse. It is supported by two soldiers of the Zimeroff Guards fully accoutred. Underneath is the Latin device - Labore et Scientia. Dr Wylie's coat of arms is unique in that it was personally designed and drawn by Czar Alexander I during his sojourn in Paris and at his special request it was confirmed by King George III of Great Britain. On the occasion of the unveiling of the statue a meeting was held in the great hall of The Academy attended by Cabinet Ministers and leading members of civic and academic life. Addresses were delivered by four distinguished guests - Dr Genochine, Professor Tchistowitch, General Suchosanet and Privy Councillor Kostoff. In memory of Wylie's sympathy for the under privileged his executors distributed a thousand roubles among the poorer students of The Academy.

Though, by his Will, he bequeathed his entire fortune to the Russian Emperor and people it was found, after a case had been raised in The Court of Chancery by his only surviving brother, Walter, that the £50,000 invested in British Government Funds along with the accrued interest could not, by British law, be alienated to a foreign power. This money became the property of his relatives among whom it was divided.

With the passing of Sir James Wylie there ended not only a life of outstanding achievement and usefulness but also what had been for a hundred and fifty years a wholly beneficent dynasty of British medical practitioners in Russia. And if, in Sir James Wylie, the Russian nation had a benefactor to whom they were deservedly grateful, we, in the Parish of Tulliallan have in him a native of whom every citizen can be unreservedly proud.

Notes

1.   William Wylie is referred to in some publications as having been The Rector of Dundee Grammar School. But this is totally erroneous. In the eighteenth century Dundee had a number of private schools, seven of which are listed in the first Dundee Directory in 1783. These schools were conducted usually in the chamber of a modest dwelling house whose owner commended himself to the local authorities, secular and ecclesiastical, as a man of good character, a regular Church attender and of sufficient learning to conduct a primary school. William Wylie was one such person and in 1796 the Town Council of Dundee "considering the character of Mr William Wylie as a teacher of English in the town of Dundee and the very favourable accounts of his services to the scholars under his charge do hereby agree to pay him Ten Guineas yearly out of the funds of the community to commence from the term of Whitsunday last. And to continue during the pleasure of the Council annerarly and that as an encouragement to him to continue his exertions which have hitherto been so useful". William Wylie was subsequently elected at Whitsunday 1804 to the Mastership of the English School, a post which he retained until his death in October 1827. (Records of The Town Council of Dundee, 1/6/96, etc.) In an alphabetical list of teachers drawn up by Dr J. W. Stephenson in his book "Education in Dundee in the eighteenth century" we find William Wylie listed as a teacher in a Private School and in The English School of which he became Master in 1804. Unlike The Grammar School, The English School was co-educational, girls being admitted as

well as boys, and the medium of education was, in all subjects, English. Situated in the Churchyard it was referred to locally as The Churchyard School and the work of the teaching staff was subject to inspection by the Town Council and the Presbytery. A new tombstone, replacing the original, bears the following inscription: "In memory of William Wylie, Teacher, born Tulliallan October 11 1766, died Dundee October 18 1827. 26 May 1856 Dr Wylie (his son) Carluke got permission to place this flat new stone". Also commemorated is his wife Annie Stupart, born 17 June 1770, died 11 August 1858 aged 88 and four members of their family, two of whom died overseas, William in Batavia and James in Russia. Of the other three brothers, all of whom are buried in Tulliallan Churchyard, George, who died at the age of 53, was in very comfortable circumstances and left cash and property to the value of almost £2000. The family business was carried on by his son - also named George. Walter and Robert were prosperous shipowners. In a list of 90 ships registered in Kincardine and owned by local citizens in 1823, two of the largest belonged to the Wylies, The Scotia valued at £1776 was Walter's, and The Jane valued at £1524 was Robert's. Robert, who died in 1844, had a son David who died in Moscow in 1836. Two of his other sons, George and Adam, were drowned at sea. Walter, the last survivor of the family, died in 1871 aged 88 years, and for a number of years owned and resided at 'Rosebank', Kincardine. His son, William, died at Rio de Janeiro in 1852. Three other deaths of Kincardine sailors took place about the same time at Rio de Janeiro from yellow fever - Captain James Stirling of the ship Constantine, William Turcan of the ship Georgina and David

Halley, mate under Walter Wylie (Alloa Advertiser, May 1, 1852).

2.   The Matriculation Records in Edinburgh University Library yield the following information: 1786 - Wylie James Anat. and Chir. 1787 - Wylie James Med. Theor and Prac. 1788 - Wylie James (Perthshire) Anat. and Chir.

3.   John and Daniel Rutherford were the grandfather and uncle respectively of Sir Walter Scott. The former studied under Boerhave at Leyden University where he was introduced to the practice of lecturing in Clinical Medicine. This he introduced at Edinburgh shortly after the 1745 Jacobite Rebellion, and it proved to be an innovation which was much appreciated by his classes. Daniel Rutherford, Professor of Botany and subsequently of Medicine, was not only an accomplished lecturer but is celebrated as the discoverer of nitrogen gas. Of him Sir Walter writes: "My uncle was a man of distinguished talents both as a chemist and a botanist and contributed by several of his researches to enlarge the bounds of science by new discoveries but he was sadly hampered by ill health which curtailed his activities" (Letters, Vol. VI, p. 83, ed. by Sir Herbert Grierson).

4.   A few years previously Robert Livingston had been banished from "the Shire of Clackmannan" for a similar offence and had been warned that if it were repeated he would become subject to the death penalty. (Sheriff Court Records of Clackmannan.)

5.   Peter's journey to Europe is the first occasion on which a Russian ruler for more than 600 years had left the

confines of his own country. It marks the division between the old exclusive, self-contained Russia and the new Russia which was to emerge as an important factor in European politics. His primary purpose in visiting Western Europe was to learn the building and management of ships with a view to establishing a Russian navy in the Black Sea. In Amsterdam he himself became a shipwright and the frigate on which the royal shipbuilder worked was for many years in the service of the East India Company. In January 1698 Peter proceeded to England. Here he worked at Deptford at shipbuilding and at the Royal Arsenal at Woolwich. In England he found so much to interest him that he continued his visit far longer than he had intended. He endeavoured - and in this he was remarkably successful - to induce skilled craftsmen to emigrate to Russia. Several hundred assented. On the night after his return from Portsmouth contracts with about sixty men concluded. These included Major van der Stamm, a leading specialist in ship designing; Captain John Perry, a hydraulic engineer; Professor Ferghasen of Aberdeen University whom he engaged to found a school of navigation at Moscow. His recruitment programme was qualitatively a remarkable success. Peter's visit to Europe convinced him of the superiority of the foreigner and to further his Westernising policy he built Petersburgh on the Baltic - "my window on the West" as he called it. Thus Peter became the father of Russian industry and all he contrived was done with a view to raising Russian society, economically and culturally, to the level of that in Western Europe, a policy which was to be continued by his successors.

Cf. Scottish Historical Review, Vol. XVIII, p. 233. "The Enticement of Scottish Artificers to Russia and Denmark 1784-86".

6.   Robert Keith Erskine - or Areskin - was the sixth son of Charles Earl of Alva and closely related to the Earl of Mar. An ardent Jacobite, he was born in 1650, studied at Oxford University where he became a Doctor of Medicine and of Philosophy. He was in the Russian Medical Service from 1690 until his death in 1718 and was Peter the Great's personal physician.

7.   "Persons calling themselves English Physicians are found in almost every town in Russia. Sometimes they have served in apothecaries' shops in Edinburgh and London but are generally Scots apothecaries who are men of professional skill and acknowledged superiority." Clarke's Travels in Russia.

8.   Werst or verst - a Russian mile - 3,500 feet in length, almost two-thirds of an English mile.

9.   Dr John Rogerson of Dumfries went to Russia in 1766, where he earned rightly a considerable reputation as a physician. Clarke in his Travels in Russia recounts how Rogerson frequently received from his grateful patients the gift of a snuff box and as regularly carried it to a jeweller for sale. The jeweller sold it again to the first nobleman who sought a suitable gift for his physician. So again and again the doctor obtained his snuff box and continued to sell it. This piece of business became so well established between the jeweller and the doctor that the snuff box was exchanged like

a bank note without a word spoken. These 'banknotes' allowed Rogerson to amass sufficient money to obtain, with some other savings, the lands of Wamphray in his native Dumfries-shire when he built the house of Dumcrieff where he died in 1823.

10.   The Emperor Paul was also suffering from a malady which was slowly destroying his reason. In the spring of 1800 Dr Rogerson wrote, "the cloud is darkening, the incoherence of his movements increases and becomes more manifest from day to day. . . . Everyone about him is at a loss what to do. Even Kutaisof is becoming very anxious." Of Alexander, Paul's son, Voroutsof, wrote, after saying that Russian was a ship whose captain had gone mad in the midst of a storm, "the second in command is a sensible quiet young man in whom the crew have confidence." Life of Catherine II, Vol. I. Tooke.

11.   Letters from the Shores of the Baltic, 1844. Letters II and III for a description of St Petersburgh; Death of the Emperor Paul, Letter XXIII. In Letter XXIV the writer describes a visit to the palace at Zarskae Selo, where the most impressive sight was the simple rooms of the late Emperor Alexander "whom all remember with affection and speak of with melancholy enthusiasm. His apartments have been kept exactly as he left them when he departed for Taganrog. His writing cabinet, a small light room with scagliola walls, seemed as if the Imperial inmate had just turned his back. There was his writing table in confusion - his well-blotted case - the pens black with ink. Through this was his simple bedroom, where in an alcove, on a slight camp bedstead with

linen coverlet, lay the fine person and troubled heart of poor Alexander. On one side was the small table with the little green Morocco looking glass - his simple English shaving apparatus - his brushes, combs - a pocket handkerchief marked Z23. On a chair lay a worn military surtout - beneath were his manly boots. There was something painful in these relics. If preserved by fraternal affection, it seems strange that the same feeling should not shield them from stranger eyes and touch."

12.   At the Battle of Borodino Sir James Wylie is credited with having attended personally to about two-hundred wounded soldiers. A vivid picture of the conditions in the medical tents is given by Tolstoy in War and Peace, Vol. II. pp. 960-968 (Penguin Edition). Section 37, p. 965, may well be the novelist's portrait of Wylie in action. Thought the Russian army was badly mauled in the battle and the casualties were enormous the Russians retained the will to resist and that is what mattered in the end.

13.   Platove or Platoff (1757-1818) - Russian soldier who showed in several campaigns such courage and capacity that he was named by Alexander I in 1801 "Hetman of the Cossacks of the Don". As such he took part in the campaigns against the French (1805-1807). After the French disaster at Leipzig he harried their retreat, gained a success at Laon and was associated with much looting. He was a good leader of irregulars, genial, daring and resourceful.

14.   William Shaw Cathcart, after a distinguished and varied military career and a spell as a representative peer in the House of Lords was appointed in 1812 by Lord

Castlereagh as British Ambassador to Russia and British Military Commissioner to the army of the Czar. Along with the British Ambassadors to Austria and Prussia he did much to maintain unity among the Allied Nations. On July 16, 1814, he was created Earl Cathcart, in appreciation of his outstanding services in securing the overthrow of Napoleon. In 1820 he relinquished his post as Ambassador to St Petersburg and much of his time, during his leisure years, was spent at Shaw Park, Alloa. Earl Cathcard died in 1843.

15.   Droska or Drosky - a low four-wheeled open carriage very popular in Russia.

16.   "This historic clock" says Ratcliffe Barnet, "after the death of Betty Wilcox was for a long time in the possession of the widow of the sailor son, who, when she became an old woman, still welcomed tourists to see it." Border By-Ways, p. 181.

17.   After a cooling off period in their friendship the Emperor Alexander came to see the necessity of resisting Napoleon if Europe were to be saved from total subjection to the French. The three years from 1805 to 1807 witnessed Napoleon's conquest of Eastern Europe as far as the Russian border. Each year saw ". . . Another deadly blow! Another mighty Empire overthrown!" Austria at the Battle of Austerlitz in 1805, Prussia at Jena in 1806 and Russia at Friedland in 1807. By the Treaty of Tilsit in June 1807 Napoleon and Alexander made peace and agreed to divide Europe between them. But Napoleon could brook no rival and continued his aggression as if no treaty had been made, just as Hitler was to do after the Treaty of Munich. Alexander then

realised - as Neville Chamberlain did - that he had been duped and now with Russia the sole unconquered country in Europe, Alexander became the leading and a most bitter antagonist of Napoleon on the continent.

18.   Autobiography by Archibald Alison, Vols I & II.

19.   The Emperor was welcomed at Canterbury by the Prince Regent as was also the King of Prussia. Both monarchs were feted and banqueted most handsomely by the Prince Regent, the Government, and by Civic and University Authorities. Wherever they went they were cheered enthusiastically by huge crowds. The Emperor's sister, the Duchess of Oldenburg, accompanied him to all the public functions and they spent as much time privately in each other's company as official engagements would permit. The Emperor had intended to travel throughout England and into Scotland as far as Edinburgh and to embark for St Petersburg from Leith. This would have provided Sir James Wylie with an opportunity to visit his native Tulliallan. But the Emperor had to curtail his visit and for Sir James that opportunity was lost. Alexander visited Oxford, staying at Merton College, and at a public meeting both he and the King of Prussia were serenaded by specially composed odes in English, Greek and Latin. Thereafter he visited Blenheim Palace, the home of Marlborough, one of Britain's greatest generals. At Portsmouth where he inspected ships of the Royal Navy and visited naval installations he was feted by enormous crowds. There he reviewed the Fleet as he was later to review the army at Portsdownhill. At the Royal Banquet hosted by the Prince Regent in honour of his two kingly guests Sir James Wylie is

listed among those present and doubtless he attended also the other official dinners and celebrations. Before leaving Pultney Hotel along with his sister the Emperor thanked Mr Escudier, the proprietor, for his attention and accommodation and Mrs Escudier was presented with a valuable brooch. The impression which Alexander left on all who met him was that of a thoroughly friendly gentleman, gracious and kindly in his manner, who had in no small measure "the common touch". On sallying out from the hotel to fulfil his engagements he was invariably confronted by a sizeable crowd of sightseers and well-wishers. Without fail he took time to shake hands with as many as possible in what we nowadays call a walkabout. At Portsmouth he captured the affection not only of the officers but of the sailors. He shared a meal with the latter on a visit to one of the ships and on another took his grog with the sailors, remarking "You call it grog. I think it very good" pouring out some for his sister who was with him. The Emperor took his farewell of the Prince Regent and Brighton before sailing from Dover to the continent - and home. - The Times, June 1814.

20.   The other Scot who had a statue in St Petersburg is Prince Barclay de Tolly, a descendant of a family who came to Russia during the time of The Revolution in 1688 from Towy (Tolly) in Aberdeenshire. Prince Barclay de Tolly was Michael by name, who distinguished himself greatly in the war with Sweden when his troops crossed the Gulf of Bothnia on ice. He became Governor of Finland. It was his policy that made the Russians retreat before the advance of Napoleon on Moscow. After the occupation of Paris, Barclay de Tolly who had been Minister for War, was made a Prince of The Russian

Empire. So in these crucial years two Scotsmen, albeit in very different roles, Wylie and Barclay served Russia and her army well. Barclay de Tolly died in 1818.

Appendices

THE ANNUAL EXPENDITURE OF THE MEDICO-CHIRURGICAL ACADEMY AT MOSCOW

	Number	Salaries *(Roubles)*	
		Each	Total
Vice President	1	Salary according to his rank provided he has no other situation	
Table Money			1,200
His Secretary	1		600
Total			**1,800**

Scientific Department

(A) Medical

	Number	Each	Total
		(Roubles)	
Professors	8	2,000	16,000
Adjuncts	8	800	6,400
Dissector	1		800
His Assistant	1		200
Experimenter	1		500
Clinical Department	-		5,000
Total			**28,900**

(B) Veterinary

	Number	Salaries *(Roubles)*	
		Each	Total
Professors	3	2,000	6,000
Adjuncts	3	800	2,400
Dissector	1		800
His Assistant	1		200
Teachers:			
Of the Russian and Latin and of Arithmetic	1		400
Writing	1		500

Smith	1	400
Assistant	1	150
Maintenance of the Veterinary Hospital for fodder, etc.		1,500
Apothecary (of the third rank)	1	250
Total		**12,600**

(C) Pharmaceutical

	Number	Salaries (Roubles)	
		Each	Total
Professor	1		2,000
Adjunct	1		800
Teacher of Latin and German	1		400
Total			**3,200**

Administration of The Scientific Department

	Number	**Salaries** *(Roubles)*	
		Each	Total
Secretary	1		1,500
Translator	1		600
Keeper of the Archives	1		400
Clerks	2	250	500
Librarian	1		700
Assistants	2	300	600
Total			**4,300**

Economical Department

	Number	Salaries (Roubles)	
		Each	Total
Inspector or Guardian of the Pupils (chosen among the medical professors)	1		1,200
Member of the Administration (chosen from the civil rank)	1		1,000
Secretary	1		600
Cashier	1		500
Book Keeper	1		400

General Expenses of the Chancery and servants			2,500
Inspector's Assistants	4	600	2,400
Commissioner	1		500
Assistant	1		300
Under Officers	2	100	200
Commissioner of the Vetinary School	1		500
His Clerk	1		150
Under Officers	2	100	200
The Swiss	1		100

Support and clothing of
the pupils of the First

Division			
Medical	200	84	16,800
Veterinary	20	84	1,680
Pharmaceutical	40	84	3,360
For Provisions		76	19,760
Classical Necessaries: books, etc...		20	5,200
Total support of the pupils of the Second Division	100	120	12,000
Crown Servants from among those unfit for active service	60	45	2,700
Grooms from Cavalry Regiments	8	50	400

Uniform of the under officers, of the grooms and of the servants		1,200
Hire of cooks, bakers, locksmiths, builders of stoves and other workmen		2,000
Manglers and washerwomen		1,000
Washing table linen and pupils' linen, for various kinds of dishes, table linen, table ware, and fodder for three work horses		1,200
Support of The Hospital for the pupils: two dressers and food for the sick		1,200
Apothecary	1	500

Assistant	1		250
Pupils	2	120	240
Fire engines, wood, lighting, cleaning chimmies, preservation of cleanliness, repairs of buildings etc...			1,500
Total			**95,140**

Besides

	Number	Salaries (Roubles)	
		Each	Total
Clergyman	1		400
Expenses of the Church and of the servants attached to it			1,000
Total			1,400
Grand Total			147,340

The constitution of both branches of the Academy - at Moscow and at Petersburgh - is every way the same.

The annual expenditure of the Petersburgh Branch amounts to - 169,300 Roubles

The annual expenditure of the Moscow Branch amounts to - 147,340 Roubles

Besides these sums 69,650 roubles common to the two Branches are expended every year in making additions to the salaries of those who have attained the title of Academic: for Pensions; for extraordinary Professors, for prizes to the students; for uniform for the pupils, on their discharge, for the increase of the libraries and of the museums, for botanical gardens, for travelling expenses and for hire of horses until the Crown provide them, etc. 69,650 Roubles

Total annual expenditure of both branches - 386,290 Roubles

The above information is given by Dr Robert Lyall in his book "The Russians"

Interviews with Sir James Wylie - 1854

In the spring of 1854 an American physician on holiday in Europe was given a letter of introduction to Sir James Wylie by Sir James Clark, a London doctor and in an article in his book A Physician's Vacation, Dr William Channing gives a lively account of his meetings with Sir James shortly before his death.

"Sir James's residence was in Galerney, a street parallel with the English Quay and directly in the rear of Madame Benson's house so that a minute's walk from where I was staying brought me to his house. I rang, enquired for Sir James and handed card and letter to the servant to deliver to his master. It seemed a very long time before I heard from above. The rooms, about which I wandered, were singularly deficient in furniture but on the walls were some pictures which to me are the best furniture. At length John appeared and asked me to follow his to Sir James. Upon entering the room my whole attention was attracted by the figure of a very tall old man between eighty and ninety stretched at full length upon a sofa. 'Let me know how I may serve you.' A desire was expressed to visit the civil and military hospitals. 'Dr ————, with the rank of Colonel, will call on you in the morning and visit all those institutions with you.'

"After this a day scarcely passed while I was in the city that I did not call on Sir James. At another visit Sir James talked of his war experiences. Among other things he spoke of the Battle of Leipzig. Moreau, who was then fighting on the side of the Allies, had both his legs shot off by a cannon ball. Sir James amputated both limbs upon the field but such was the shock that Moreau had received from the ball that he died but a few hours after the operation. It was in that battle that he was made a baronet with the privilege of armorial bearings. He told the servant to bring him the patent of his baronetcy signed by the English monarch which it was evident he was happy to show me. In connection with this was a display of all the decorations and orders which he had received from the many monarchs he had served. I told Sir James of my purpose to go to Moscow. He said he would give me letters, which he afterwards did, to His Excellency Professor Fischer, the head of the Russian Bureau of National Sciences and to Doctor Pfachl, principal medical officer of the great Military Hospital in Moscow.

"Upon another occasion something was said which carried him back to his boyhood and his servant was ordered to bring him a certain package which was very carefully opened and its contents showed to me. 'Here,' said Sir James, 'are my school books. My first writing books, my cyphering books, and these are my mathematical manuscripts. You see, I have kept them all.' They were in perfect preservation and arranged after the order of time. The writing was excellent and the neatness of them all showed how early had been formed the habit of doing well what he had done. Here was an old man between eighty and ninety and here were the records of his earliest days. Something was said of the interest which would be taken in the history of such a life. Sir James said he had written a work in many volumes of every important event in which he had taken part. It was finished for the press but he thought it his duty to the Czar to tell him what he had done. Nicholas begged him to destroy it, and with so much emphasis was the request made that he promised to comply - and had performed his promise. The record of a long life which had been spent in the active and responsible service of three monarchs and in the most important portions of Russian history, which in fact, embraced most literally the whole existence of that Empire, was in a moment destroyed. The evidence which had just been showed me in the minutest details of the care in which he had preserved the earliest records of his life, the intellectual habits of this old man abundantly showed how well fitted he was for just such a work as he had described to me. The regret was expressed at the loss of such an autobiography. The answer was, 'The Emperor had directed it' and he obeyed the command. Sir James expressed again and again his regard, his reverence, his affection for the Emperor. It was clear that confidence had been reposed in him and that he lay under great obligations to Nicholas.

"I was told that Sir James was very rich, his property being between five and six millions roubles silver. I asked who would be his heir. 'The Emperor', was the reply. He has left his whole property to him. Sir James gave me copies of his published works. Among these was a thick volume on the Materia Medica of Russia.

"The day before I left St Petersburgh I called to make my visit of leave. I found him very ill. He had passed a wretched night and was breathing with so much agony, and was so exhausted that he could hardly raise his hand to me or say farewell. He was stretched out on the sofa, as he was when I first saw him, and it seemed impossible that he would ever rise from it again. I thanked him for all the kindness he had showed me and took my leave. It was not without sadness this leave-taking at the borders of the grave."

The above is quoted in The Alloa Advertiser, 7th March 1857. The Editor prefaced the above excerpt from Channing's book with the comment that "had Sir James Wylie left his wealth to his native town instead of to the Russian Emperor who already had an abundance of riches, our neighbourhood might have been enriched with another charity like that of MacNab's famous in the annals of Dollar."

Through Russian Eyes

A letter from the Russian Correspondent of The London Daily Telegraph enclosing an article in the Vedomostee which, he says, will be equally interesting to Russians and English. The article gives details of the unveiling of a handsome bronze monument in honour of Sir James Wylie.

"On 25th December 1859 the Medico-Chirurgical Academy of St Petersburgh celebrated the inauguration of a monument in honour of its first President, Doctor and Privy Councillor James Wylie, one of the greatest administrative geniuses in the organisation of schools for medical instruction and to whose exertions are not only due the present flourishing state of the Academy but the development of medical science all over the empire. The life and activity of Wylie present a picture of unexampled excellence in the history of Russia and the fact of no biography having yet been published of this truly great man shall not prevent us from attempting a sketch of his memorable life.

"Having come here in the simple capacity of a medical man, a graduate of the University of Edinburgh and possessing a higher degree of scientific knowledge than had ever been attained in Russia prior to his arrival in the country, he applied himself with the whole force of his powerful mind to raise the standard of the profession and to establish a number of schools for the propagation of a science almost unknown, and while thus exerting himself for the good of a foreign nation he nevertheless during the whole of his life not only remained a

British subject but a true son of his native country: never however giving the slightest occasion for doubting the sincerity of his sentiments towards his adopted land. Even this praise, high as it is, does not meet the whole of his desserts. Not satisfied with devoting his life to the prosecution of a grand aim he carried his anxiety for the good of Russia to the time when he should no longer be of this world.

"In his Will he left half a million of roubles for the construction of a great St Petersburgh hospital to be attended by the pupils of the Medico-Chirurgical Academy. Thus he died as he had lived, the benefactor of his race. His merits, which his contemporaries did not fail to acknowledge, have now received a lasting memorial in the shape of the Statue just erected in the great court of the Imperial Medico-Chirurgical Academy.

"The monument represents Dr Wylie seated on a rock and attired in the parade uniform of a military surgeon with a brilliant display of orders on his breast. At his feet lies his well-known work on 'Military Pharmacy', while the left hand holding a paper scroll and the right grasping a pencil show him in the attitude of penning his thoughts on the organisation of medical institutions in Russia. The proportions of the figure are colossal. The material is bronze, the pedestal, for which black Finland granite has been selected, is adorned with caryatides emblematic of Hygeia the goddess of health. The four sides of the pedestal contain respectively the late doctor's coat of arms superbly executed in bronze; a representation of the first sitting of the Academy; Wylie's activity in the field during the years 1813, 1814 and 1815; and the dedicatory inscription. Other bas-reliefs illustrate the high degree of perfection to which the institution has attained and the glory and honour which it is designed to impart to the whole class of military surgeons in Europe.

"The Doctor's coat of arms consist of a shield divided horizontally into two parts. In the upper portion 'OR', the Imperial Coat of Arms of Russia is inserted; while the lower department, 'GULES', shows a silver sword below which is drawn an open hand and two five-pointed stars. The shield is crowned with an open nobility helmet, surmounted by a Cossack of the Don in the act of jumping from his horse. It is supported by two soldiers of the Zimeroff Guards fully accoutred. Under it appears the Latin device - 'Labore et scientia'. Dr Wylie's coat of arms is remark- able as being the design of the Emperor Alexander I himself. The Czar, during his sojourn in Paris in 1814 having resolved to reward the merits of the doctor added to the distinction by presenting him with an armorial drawing from his own hand which, in the pursuance of the latter's request, was confirmed by George III of England.

"The monument was inaugurated on the 25th of December in honour of the anniversary of the day on which in the year 1790 Dr Wylie entered the Russian service, in the capacity of surgeon in ordinary to the Jeletski Regiment. The solemnity which took place in the great hall of the Academy was attended by the ministers and many of the leading personages in the various departments of the public service. Dr Genochine made a speech in honour of the founder of the institution: Professor Tchistowitsch following him and extolling the merits of their first president in the name of the present professors of the Academy. To these orators succeeded General Suchosanet and Privy Councillor Kosloff as representatives of the War Department who spoke highly of the eminent military services rendered by the deceased. Thus terminated a solemnity full of significance for the present as well as for the future generations - a solemnity in honour of a man of the greatest excellence and of the most commanding talents.

"We must not, however, omit mentioning a circumstance in connection with this memorial which is in harmony with the whole tendency of the doctor's life. Desirous of perpetuating the name of their ancestor by good deeds, his executors, on the day of the inauguration of the statue, presented the sum of a thousand roubles, to be divided among the poorer students of the Academy. Thus the festival intended for the reward of past services was at the same time an occasion for incitement to future distinction."

In sending the above excerpt from the Russian newspaper the correspondent of The Daily Telegraph adds this personal reflection: "In perusing these lines I could not help thinking that whatever may be the present tenor of thought in this country with respect to England, it is satisfactory to perceive that latent animosity does not prevent the Russians from heartily recognising the merits of a native of Great Britain."

Sir James Wylie's Will

When Sir James Wylie died in the spring of 1854 Walter was his only surviving brother. But each of the others left a family, so there were many relatives who hoped to receive a share of his very considerable fortune which was reckoned to be about a million pounds. The Crimean War broke out later that year and as Britain and Russia were engaged in hostilities no information about his affairs was readily available. His brother waited for a year and then applied for Letters of Administration. Information was received that Sir James had made a Will on 10th February 1854. In it he ordered certain houses in St Petersburgh belonging to him to be sold, "with all their household establishments and articles thereto pertaining". His estates at New Ladogo and at Schluseburgh with their peasants, "excepting those serfs who for their faithful services he might set free" - and also the woodlands with farms and all "the economical establishments thereon" were likewise to be sold. The next part of his Will is as follows: "The money proceeds of the above, as also my capital which shall remain with me after my death in ready money and in bank billets belonging to me shall be divided into ten equal parts. Two of them I destine to be employed in arranging for me a respectable funeral and erecting a monument to me, and in such acts of charity to my memory as my executors shall think proper. Of the remaining eight parts I intend making afterwards a detailed disposal; but if from any cause I make no such disposal of the capital assigned for these eight parts or of any fractions thereof then the sums which will thus remain indisposed of by me I most humbly lay at the feet of His Imperial Majesty, my most gracious master, The Emperor of all the Russias, and I venture to express the wish that the sum may be employed in memory of my most august benefactors of Blessed Memory; The Emperor Paul Petrovich and Alexander Pavlovitch and the Grand Duke Michael Pavlovitch for some establishments of public or charitable benefit which shall bear my name." He appointed three executors of his Will, revoked all earlier settlements and declared that all his property, of whatever kind, was his own and had been honestly acquired by himself. No one had any right to interfere with the dispositions he had made nor with any acts of his executors. He made no reference as to how any residue should be used, and he concluded his Will with these sentences: "Having reached the decline of years and drawing near the term of human existence, I am ready to meet my dying hour, resigned to the will of Providence, with a calm mind and a clear conscience. Recalling to mind the course of my past life, I can say from my own convictions, without any pride that in the sphere of my activity I behaved and fulfilled my duties conscientiously and honestly not without advantage to Russia. More than sixty years I was in the service of three monarchs of Russia and every commission bestowed upon me I fulfilled with real ardour and steady devotedness. I laboured unremittingly for the organisation of the medical department and for the education of physicians in Russia as my second native country, and the thought that my endeavours have not been unsuccessful is not a vain consolation in the last days of my life. I deeply feel all the favours with which I have been loaded by my most august benefactors and the high confidence they bestowed upon me, and this feeling I preserved reverently in my heart to the last moment of my life. I beseech the Almighty that He may save Russia, her wise monarch and the Imperial family. Almighty God! Grant my prayer! and when my last hour shall come, receive indulgently my soul."

On the 10th February 1854 he "completed and explained" his Will, directing that the eight parts of the capital should be employed in commemoration of the late Grand Duke Michael Pavlovitch for the erection of an hospital in St Petersburgh to be called "The Hospital of the Saint Archangel Michael founded by The Baronet Wylie".

No specific reference was made in his Will to the £50,000 which he had invested in British Government Funds at 3%, which with the accrued interest now exceeded £67,000. Walter Wylie on behalf of himself and the other relatives, some twenty-five in number, disputed the claim of the executors of Sir James's Will that this money belonged to the Russian Emperor and nation. As two different legal systems were involved and as Britain and Russia were at war it took a long time for the Chancery Court in London to reach a determination in the dispute, "a large army of counsel of the greatest eminence being enlisted on each side". The verdict was given in favour of Walter Wylie and his associates but the executors appealed to the Lord Justices who upheld the decision of the lower court. The executors were still not satisfied and lodged an appeal with The House of Lords which was heard in March 1862. They issued their judgment on 3rd April in favour of the claims of the next of kin on which day "a telegram reached Alloa with the news". Among the beneficiaries entitled to a share of the £67,000 were the following: Mr Walter Wylie (brother); Mrs James Neish, Dundee; Rev John Wylie, Carluke; Mrs Alexander Edward, Dundee; Miss Janet Meiklejohn Wylie, Dundee; Miss Ann Wylie of Rose Angle, Dundee; The Rev. Francis Wylie, Elgin; Mr George Wylie, St Andrews; Mrs Jean Cabel, Dundee; Mrs Alex Luke, Culross, Perthsire; Mrs Haldane Wylie, Kincardine.

The following comment on the hearing of the case by The House of Lords is interesting: "In the appeal before The House of Lords the discussion did not really turn upon the words of the Will at all but on a point raised by the wily Lord Chancellor for the first time and never thought of in the courts below; whether by Russian law the simple nomination did not give them all the property not specially disposed of by the testator which was the old Common Law both of England and Scotland. In the absence of any document indicating what the intention of Sir James Wylie was as to the money invested in the British Funds the Court of last resort decided in favour of the next of kin."

. . . "The Scottish physician by all accounts seems always to have cherished very friendly feelings towards his own kindred, and it can scarcely be supposed that he would have overlooked them at his death: but it is a fortunate circumstance that the highest tribunal of his native country has pronounced a verdict in accordance with what any one would conceive to have been the wishes of a man at the close of a long life whose natural feelings towards his own flesh and blood had not altogether decayed" (Editorial comment in The Alloa Advertiser).

In his submission to the House of Lords, Mr John Boyd Baxter, solicitor, Dundee, deponed that through his agent in St Peters- burgh he laid a case for opinion before two sworn advocates of that city of great reputation for their skill and learning in the laws of Russia. But when these gentlemen found that the late Emperor of Russia was mentioned in the Will and that the present Czar might or might not be interested in it they declined giving any written opinion on the case, their opinion being in favour of the next of kin and therefore unfavourable to the possible interests of the Emperor.

Mr Baxter believes that they would have run the risk of injury by the authorities if their names were disposed in any opinion inimical to the supposed interest of the Emperor.

Opinion in an A : B case was stated and the opinions of Russian advocates was obtained favourable to the next of kin, though in Russia, as in England, learned gentlemen appear to have been found who entertained upon a case stated by the other side an entirely opposite opinion.

The Alexander Legend

After the death of their pious and revered Emperor Alexander a legend grew up, and still persists, that he did not die at Taganrog on the Sea of Azov coast on 19th November 1825 but that, world weary and depressed, he wished to renounce the throne by feigning death. The Empress, Sir James Wylie and one or two others, it is said, were admitted to the secret. A chasseur who was accidentally killed provided an ideal alibi. He was put into the coffin. Alexander boarded surreptitiously an English vessel and was conveyed to Siberia. There he led the life of a hermit and died in 1864. What appears to be the case is that some eleven years after the Czar's death at Taganrog an unknown wanderer arrived in Northern Siberia wearing peasant's clothes and closely resembling Alexander in appearance. He refused to give any information about himself. He claimed to be a man of God. He won respect on account of his manner of life, education and culture. He had a knowledge of several languages and in tales he recounted about Napoleon and the Royal Court he seemed to have had inside knowledge. Dame Rumour said he was visited by members of the Royal Family in darkness. The evidence for the truth of the legend is far from satisfactory and over against it there is the written account of the Emperor's illness, the autopsy, and death by a man of Sir James Wylie's standing and character. One item seems to give colour to the legend. The sarcophagus when opened in the Peter-Paul Fortress was found to be empty. Either a corpse had never lain in it or was removed. But in the absence of more specific evidence one should at least suspend judgment or attribute the legend to the Russian love of myth.

Sir James Dewar

Figure 4: Sir James Dewar, from a portrait by his nephew, Dr Thomas W. Dewar, M.D.

Nature

We are surrounded and embraced by her, we are powerless to separate ourselves from her and powerless to penetrate beyond her. We obey her laws even when we rebel against them.

Gothe

What Science Says To Truth

As is the mainland to the sea
       Thou art to me:
Thou standest stable, while against thy feet
       I beat, I beat!

Yet from they cliffs so sheer, so tall
       Sands crumble and fall;
And golden grains of my tides each day
       Carry away.

William Watson

The production of cold is a thing very worthy of enquiry both for the use and the disclosure of causes. For heat and cold are nature's two hands whereby she chiefly worketh.

Francis Bacon

Some Of The Honours Conferred Upon Sir James Dewar

•   Hon. LL.D. from all four Scottish Universities - St Andrew's, Glasgow, Aberdeen and Edinburgh. He is the only person to have been so honoured.

•   F.R.S.E. - Fellow of The Royal Society of Edinburgh (1873). (http://www.ma.hw.ac.uk/RSE/)

•   F.R.S. - Fellow of The Royal Society (1877).

•   D.Sc. of the University of Victoria, Dublin, London, Brussels and Christiana.

•   Ph.D. - Honorary Doctor of Natural Philosophy, Freiburg University, Germany (1911).

•   Gunning Victoria Jubilee Prize of The Royal Society of Edinburgh (1893).

•   Rumford Medal of The Royal Society (1894)

•   Lavoisier Medal of The French Academy. The first occasion on which it was awarded to a British subject. (http://www.sfc.fr)

•   Queen Victoria's Diamond Jubilee. Jubilee Medals were awarded to eminent citizens in various walks of life. One of those so recognised was Professor James Dewar.

• Hodgkins Gold Medal of Smithsonian Institute. U.S.A. The first time it was awarded for scientific work to anyone outside the United States - conferred upon Professor De- war "for his researches on the liquefaction of air". (1899). (http://www.si.edu/)

• Appointed The Bakerian Lecturer to the Royal Society for 1901. The subject of his lecture was - "The Nadir of Temperature and allied problems".

• Elected President of The British Association for the Advancement of Science, 1902 - one of the highest honours which can be conferred on a British Scientist. Professor Dewar was elected also to the presidency of several scientific societies. (http://www.britassoc.org.uk)

• Knighthood conferred on Professor Dewar, 1905.

• La Societa Italiana della Scienze, the President of which was Professor Cannizzaro, had awarded The Matteucci Medal for 1906 to Sir James Dewar. The medal is given for the most important work in physics whether Italian or foreign - The Times, July 1906. (http://www.accademiaxl.it/)

• Elected Corresponding Member of The Academy of Sciences. Copenhagen (1907).

• Elected Foreign Member of The National Academy of Science, Washington (1907). (http://www.nas.edu/)

• Elected an Honorary Member of The German Chemical Society (1908). (http://www.gdch.de/)

•   Elected a member of The Belgian Academy of Literature and the Fine Arts in the section Mathematics and The Physical Sciences (1908).

•   On 11th February 1899 at Marlborough House, the Prince of Wales in the presence of the Council of the Royal Society of Arts presented The Albert Medal to Sir James Dewar for "his investigations into the liquefaction of gases and the properties of matter at low temperatures, investigation which have resulted in the production of the lowest temperatures yet reached, the use of vacuum vessels for the thermal isolation and the application of cooled charcoal to the separation of gaseous mixtures and to the production of high vacua". - The Times. (http://www.rsa.org.uk/rsa/index.asp)

•   The Academia dei Lincei elected Sir James Dewar a Foreign Member, with the approval of His Majesty the King of   Italy   (1910). (http://galileo.imss.firenze.it/museo/a/eaccail.html)

•   Awarded The Copley Medal by The Royal Society - for his research (1916). (http://www.royalsoc.ac.uk/)

•   Elected an Honorary Member of The Institute of Civil Engineers. (http://www.ice.org.uk)

•   Awarded The Silver Medal of The Chemical Industry of Great Britain, "in recognition of his conspicuous services which by his research work in both pure and applied science he has rendered to The Chemical Industry" (1918).

•   "The Franklin Medal has been awarded to Sir James Dewar by The Franklin Institute of Philadelphia, in recognition of his numerous and most important contributions to our knowledge of physical and chemical phenomena and his great skill and inventive genius in attacking and solving chemical and physical problems of the first magnitude" - The Times, April 1919.

• The Earl of Reading, The British Ambassador, was invited by The Franklin Institute to receive the medal on Sir James's behalf. It was the first award of the medal to a British subject. In handling over the medal Principal Kellar spoke of Sir James's "unparalleled record of industry and achievement in pure science and of his two most famous inventions, the Dewar flask and, with Sir Frederick Abel, cordite, which had been a most potent factor in fighting successfully the War, 1914-18. (http://sln.fi.edu/)

Biography

In the 1760s Thomas Dewar left the small rural community at Overtoun, where his forebears had for long been resident, to commence business as a vintner in the rapidly expanding town of Kincardine. The new venture prospered and the Unicorn Inn, often referred to as Dewar's Inn, became the principal tavern in the parish. There, on 20th September 1842, James Dewar, who was to become an experimental chemist of world renown, was born to the great grandson of the founder of the business, who was also named Thomas, and his wife Agnes Eadie (Note 1). James was their sixth son and the youngest member of the family. The Dewars, one of whom became a Bailie, were highly respected in the community and were frequently called upon to witness legal documents such as wills and sasines, their inn being a recognized venue for property and other goods. The family were staunch members of The Auld Licht Kirk. His father, James tells us, was a man of marked originality and character and was an active member of the Board of Management of the local United Presbyterian Congregation in whose affairs he evinced a keen interest (Note 2). His Presbyterianism was transmitted to his famous son of whom an intimate colleague, Professor H. E. Armstrong, said, "The son was true to the breed; was ever a presbyter". Besides conducting the routine business of the inn Thomas Dewar also catered for local functions, such as the annual dinner of the Horticultural Society, where his standard of catering and service was invariably highly commended (Note 3). He was a keen amateur naturalist and, possessing also a bent for engineering, by a self-constructed plant he installed gas into his house and inn when it was quite unknown in the neighbourhood (Note 4). After The Kincardine Light & Gas Company, in which he bought shares, became suppliers of gas to the town, he dispensed with his private plant in favour of receiving supplies from that Company and disposed of his equipment. Little is known about James's early years in Kincardine. He attended the New Subscription School (Note 5) where, in 1852, as a pupil in the second top class he gained with 81% the second prize and was awarded also a prize in drawing. His schooling was interrupted by a long illness; he having contracted rheumatic fever as a result of his falling through the ice, in consequence of which he had to go about on crutches for two years and his lungs were so weakened that he was forced to abandon playing the flute at which he had become quite proficient. At his golden wedding celebrations he remarked in jocular vein that it had been his ambition at that time to become a professional musician. To bring some cheer and variety into the young invalid's monotonous days, which were spent chiefly in reading, his father engaged the services of the local fiddler who not only entertained James but also taught him to play. Having stuck up a friendship with the local joiner James acquired the art of making fiddles, a skill at which he became quite expert and he often remarked in later life that his manual dexterity, which was the envy of many of his colleagues, sprang from those early years when, as a boy, he tried his prentice hand at fiddle making. Several of his fiddles found their way into the homes of local families and for a number of years were seen about the town. But there was one which he labelled "James Dewar – 1854" in boyish imitation of the practice of Stradivari who signed his violins and about whom twelve-year-old James had been reading at the time. The prank he recalled with puckish humour when that violin was played to good effect by two young ladies after he and Lady Dewar had received a golden wedding present from the members of the Royal Institution in August 1921. During his two years' convalescence James, who was a voracious reader, laid the foundation of what was to become his extraordinarily wide knowledge of English literature and his life-long love of good books. But his particular interest was given to arithmetic and mathematics. By 1858 James had so far outstripped his teacher in these disciplines that "the teacher had to prepare for the pupil", which was a far from satisfactory state of affairs. In that year the sixteen-year-old boy, whose mother had died in 1852, had to face also the sad, traumatic experience of his father's death which took place on 2nd September 1857, and which resulted in the almost immediate break-up of the family home. Now, James was an orphan with no home of his own. Alexander, one of his older brothers who for a short time had been a teacher in the Subscription School, was to become a medical student at Edinburgh University. None of the others were interested in carrying on the large business which their father had pursued with considerable success. The Unicorn Inn or Hotel, which was also a well-known posting house, with its entire equipment, furnishings, coach houses and stables was put on the market at the end of September (Note 6). For James the schoolboy, it must have been a very trying and unsettling time and one is not surprised that, in all the circumstances, he was reluctant to continue at the local school. He appears to have made his home with his brother Robert Menzies who in that year had commenced business in the town as a draper and who showed a kindly interest in his youngest brother. Fortunately James had in his minister, the Rev. Andrew Gardiner, in whose church his father had been an office-bearer and who was a close family friend and who was also a trustee in the late Thomas Dewar's estate, a wise and kind counsellor. Himself, "a classical scholar of no mean order", Mr Gardiner appreciated the outstanding ability of his young charge and persuaded him to go for a year to The Dollar Institution and not without some difficulty did he also persuade his co-trustees to make available the funds necessary for the lad's maintenance as a boarder at the school. There, in the house of Dr Lindsay, he found an excellent "home from home" under the supervision of a genial Christian man and also, in Dr Lindsay the dominie, a superb mathematician and an unusually brilliant teacher under whose tuition James was to make most remarkable progress. Nothing finer could have happened to the boy. Between teacher and pupil a very close bond of friendship grew up. James Dewar was spoken of as "the doctor's favourite pupil" and the pupil cherished a life-long sense of gratitude to his mentor. When, in 1907, he returned to his former school, now as Sir James Dewar and a scientist of European renown, he began his address to the pupils with a eulogy of Dr Lindsay "under whose roof it had been my great good fortune to reside and who could only be described as a great man. It was entirely due to his influence and under his direction that my bent in life was directed toward the side which it has been" – and then he added with his customary modesty when speaking about himself – "and probably the only side where I should have succeeded". Nor was he alone in appreciating Dr Lindsay's knowledge and teaching skill. Sir David Gill, one year senior to James at school and later to become Astronomer Royal at Capetown, had this to say about Dr Lindsay's method of instruction; "I shall never forget my first lesson in Euclid. My word, that was a revelation! . . . We were taken through the whole axioms in Euclid and asked to deny them if we could. Lindsay made us feel as if we were finding out things for ourselves and that we were really growing Euclids that might advance to knowledge. There was at once a strong practical interest in the whole business. So it came about that the whole thing was one of deepest interest to us from beginning to end. In chemistry it was extraordinary how, absolutely without a laboratory, he continued to instruct us in it. Lindsay got hold of me and all my soul was wrapt up in him and what he had to teach me." In James Dewar's time John Milne was the Rector. "Dignified, genial, immaculately dressed and always a perfect gentleman", says a former pupil, "he occasionally taught the classics and did it well". There was Mr Kirk, a man of wide erudition, who taught Latin but who knew also several other languages including Hebrew and Hindustani (Note 7). Dr Clyde, who later went to Edinburgh Academy where he taught Latin and Greek, was a charming man who at Dollar taught French, German and Italian. Mr Douglas, who had succeeded Mr Peter Steven as writing master in 1855, was known to the pupils as "Black John". He was swarthy of countenance and inky of finger and though an excellent instructor he had a most irascible temper. His house was exactly opposite Dr Lindsay's and on dark winter nights the boarders in Dr Lindsay's house would tie a long thin string, which was carried across the street from the window of their boarding house, to the knocker of Black John's door. Then, a knock would be heard at the door. A servant would open it to find no one there. Another knock followed, with similar consequences and yet another, until Black John himself would emerge in a tearing rage and rush around the garden looking for the culprit among the buses, to the delighted amusement of the boys opposite who remained quite unsuspected – James Dewar, one imagines, being among "the innocents"! Reflecting on his schooldays, Sir James, who presided on Thursday, 24th May 1906, at the first "Old Dollar Boys' Dinner" south of the Tweed, in the Great Central Hall in London, said of his teachers: "They were not only teachers but men to whom the pupils could look back with confidence for guidance and example in the broader issues of life." His brief career at The Dollar Institution terminated on 3rd August 1859 when the annual examination, attended by external examiners, took place to be followed by the prize-giving. The two principal examiners were Professors Pillans and Kelland. Among the visitors, whose presence was recorded in the local newspapers, were the Rev. Andrew Gardiner and Messrs Duncan Wright, the well-known Kincardine shipbuilder, and James's brother Robert who had a drapery business in Kincardine. It must have been a proud occasion for the Kincardine trio, for by far and away the most outstanding pupil in the school was James Dewar. The catalogue of the awards he won is impressive. Here they are: Mechanical drawing – 3rd Prize; geometry (senior) – 1st Prize; algebra – 2nd Prize; experimental philosophy – 1st Prize; chemistry – 1st Prize; mineralogy and geology – 1st Prize; physical geography – 3rd Prize; human physiology, laws of health and zoology – 2nd Prize. The mathematical medal – 1st equal James Dewar and Playford Reynolds. In a statement at the prize giving Principal Milne said that "James Dewar was by his scholarship entitled to the medal and would have got it but for a law of the Institution which declares that no one can receive it unless he has attended the Academy for two sessions, and as he had attended but one, it was awarded to the other boy". Commenting on the examinees in the mathematical classes Professor Kelland spoke of the exceedingly creditable performance of all the boys, "more especially as regarded one lad who had scarcely any knowledge of mathematics, yet, through only one session at school he showed abilities which might well have been the labour of three years (Note 8). James Dewar was not only a lad of quite exceptional ability but a dedicated student, as he was to prove to be also at the university where a fellow student said of him that "he used to sit up half the night in pursuit of his studies".

With the completion of his short but distinguished career at Dollar in August 1859 he did not cease to be interested in his old school, nor did it forget him. With justifiable pride there was duly chronicled in the Dollar Magazine the plethora of honours, which came to their former pupil as year succeeded year and in 1907 the magazine carried this intimation: "We are glad to learn that Sir James Dewar promised to be present at the academy exhibition on 27th June and to give a lecture on his great discovery, liquefied air, accomplished with the nadir of temperature – 443 Fahrenheit of frost." Let the Rector, Mr Dougall, report the occasion: "The big hall was packed, as it never was packed before, to hear him describe the wonderful properties of liquid air and to see him actually reduce the air of Dollar to a liquid state. In the course of the lecture Sir James seized an India rubber ball. Suddenly turning to the wall he threw it forcibly and to the delight of everyone he brought off a low catch. Then, once more resuming a serious attitude, he dipped the ball into the liquid and again threw it; and to everyone's astonishment it smashed on the wall to atoms." The magazine article which describes the event, ends with these sentences: "To the uninitiated the lecture was fascinating in the extreme. Even to those deeply versed in scientific matters it seemed to open up a fairy world, the genius of which had taken up residence in a liquid, BOILING at a temperature far beyond zero. Truly he was no uncertain genius under the control of such a magician as a successor of Michael Faraday." After the lecture Lady Dewar presented to the Academy an attractive statuette, about twelve inches high, of Sir James in his London laboratory holding aloft a vessel of liquid air, which was accepted by Mr Dougall and which is still today one of the school's treasured possessions. Thereafter, Sir James and Lady Dewar went to the Library Hall for lunch where he had an opportunity of meeting and conversing with some who were his contemporaries at school. But more important and of much more enduring value to the school was the conversation which he had with the mangers in which he urged them in the strongest terms to provide laboratory accommodation for the teaching of science. A genius like Dr Lindsay might be able to teach chemistry from a book and inspire a few of his listeners to pursue their study of the subject at a university but without a laboratory, Sir James insisted, that was well-nigh impossible. The seed fell on good ground and to their credit the managers gave to his advice the weight it merited. New laboratories, toward the building of which Sir James gave £110, were erected at a cost of £5,000 and were in use two years later. In 1912 he gave a donation, the most generous in the list of contributions, of £20 to The Tennis Court Fund, and in 1919, when the school was celebrating its centenary, he added to his message of congratulations a cheque for £100, all of which verifies the remark he made in a letter accompanying the photograph, taken in 1902 by Dr A. Scott in the laboratory of The Royal Institution and sent in response to a request from the school, in which he said, "anything I could do to show my appreciation of my Academy career would be a real pleasure", adding with his usual modesty, "all the same I think you are making too much of my work". As a member and first president of The London Old Boys' Club and as a regular subscriber to The Dollar Magazine he kept in touch with his school, grateful not only for the instruction he had received but also for the idyllic environment in which the school is set. "How we all, as boys, used to visit the Glen and Castle Campbell and at the old pile endeavour to relate the exact spot where John Knox dispensed the Sacrament within its walls - and Sheriffmuir, and the rambles over the Ochills and the strolls long the banks of the winding Devon of which Burns sang so sweetly." At the time of his death in 1923 appropriate tributes were paid to his memory in The Dollar Magazine and at a meeting of The Committee of Management of the school by Mr Malcolm the chairman. In reply to a letter of sympathy Lady Dewar wrote: "He always retained great affection for his old school and all its happy memories and it was ever a joy to him to hear of the continued success of Dollar Academy."

"His bright and brief career" at the school over, James, now 17, matriculated as a student in 1859 at Edinburgh University which he attended until 1862 when he stood high in the list of those who gained First Class Honours in chemistry and also won the prize for written answers to questions on the professor's lectures in a competition open to the whole class. With justifiable pride the rector reported at the prize giving ceremonies at The Dollar Institution in 1860 and 1861 the prizes which had been awarded at the university to James Dewar and in 1862 his achievement as a first class honours graduate. From the evidence of books in his library we know what some of these awards were. In mathematics under Professor Kelland he gained, in 1860, the first prize in the second class, a success which he repeated in the following year. In 1861 he took also the first prize in the second division of the natural philosophy class and along with it an award for "Eminent Success" in the same subject under Professor P. Guthrie Tait who had succeeded Professor J. D. Forbes in 1860 and in whose laboratory James had worked in 1859 and "whom he always held in reverent memory". "In these days" wrote Dr J. Y. Buchanan, one of his student contemporaries, "James Dewar could master any subject he had a will to master." He also attended the chemistry class under Professor Lyon Playfair who had succeeded William Gregory in 1858. Unlike his predecessors Playfair appreciated the importance of students being provided with adequate instruction through practical experiments as well as by lectures. So, he founded a laboratory in the Chemistry Department and as the number of students attending his classes made it impossible for him to give practical instruction to them all, he introduced a tutorial system using some of his ablest students to pass on to small groups the instruction which he had given to them. One of the tutors was James Dewar. This brought him into close contact with Playfair who soon realised his exceptional skill as an experimenter and who, we are told, urged James to enter the dyestuffs industry where his talents would earn him the status and income he deserved. But in this matter the student did not follow his professor's advice. On 4th February 1867, Professor Playfair read to the Royal Society of Edinburgh a paper by James Dewar Esq. on the "oxidation of Phenyl Alcohol and a mechanical arrangement adapted to illustrate structure in the non-saturated Hydrocarbons", Dewar himself being not yet a member of the Society; to which he was elected on 15th February 1869. The printing of this paper in The Proceedings of the Royal Society marks the first publication from the pen of James Dewar in the field of scientific research and is the forerunner of a multitude of such papers, whose name is legion, published over the next half century. Between professor and student a close friendship developed and Playfair was one of the guests at James's wedding in 1871. In his autobiography the professor wrote: "I may claim with some pride that many eminent chemists have been evolved from my teaching, among whom Professor Dewar of Cambridge is conspicuous." Many years later, on 9th June 1896, a reception was held by The Chemical Society, of which James Dewar was that year's president, to honour the seven past presidents who had attained their jubilee as members of the Society. In his letter of invitation to Lord Playfair, as the professor had now become, James wrote, "All the foreign members have been invited as well as a number of distinguished guests who are interested in the progress of chemistry and anxious to do honour to the past presidents". Sadly, Lord Playfair died in May, a month before the dinner took place and in a letter of sympathy to his widow James Dewar wrote of his "lifelong veneration for the departed. He was my master in everything. I owe all to him. His memory will ever remain with me as one of the abiding treasures of my life."

Fortunately for James and his brother Alexander, who had become a student at Edinburgh University and with whom, when he followed to the university, James shared lodgings as paying guests in the home of two elderly ladies, with whom James continued to stay until his marriage in 1871, their father had left sufficient money to provide for their education. In his Will, made on 21st May 1857, Mr Dewar's assets in cash exceeded £1,657, quite a substantial sum in these days. To this there fell to be added the value of The Unicorn Inn, several house properties in Kincardine, some shares in The Kincardine Light and Gas Company along with the grain crops in several fields. By the terms of his Will, his six sons shared equally in their father's estate. Those who had reached their majority were paid their shares outright. Those who were still in their minority were to receive their portion as soon as they became twenty- one, with the proviso that in the meantime the trustees were empowered "to use what they deemed requisite towards their maintenance and education, so long as they were minors". The three trustees were Rev. Andrew Gardiner, minister of the United Presbyterian Church in Kincardine; Alexander Dewar, brother of the deceased, wine and spirit merchant in Leith and Ebenezer Mill, S.S.C.

On the completion of his course at the university James Dewar became assistant, with special responsibility for practical demonstrations to the medical students to Professor Crum Brown who had succeeded Playfair in the Chair of Chemistry. Once again the senior discerned the outstanding ability of his junior. Dr Crum Brown believed that chemistry would eventually become as exact a science as mathematics and he was very interested in the application of mathematics to chemistry. He suggested a more convenient scheme for the representation of the structure of compounds than the one invented by the Belgian chemist Kekulé. In 1867 James Dewar invented a mechanical device to represent Crum Brown's new graphic notation for organic compounds and this, having fallen into Playfair's hands, was transmitted by him to Kekulé, who in turn invited Dewar to spend a summer semester at his laboratory in Ghent. So it became the young scientist's great good fortune to make the acquaintance of one of the most brilliant chemists in Europe. Many years later James Dewar was one of the signatories to a letter to his fellow scientists soliciting contributions for the erection of a memorial to Kekulé which resulted in the fine statue in bronze at the Chemical Institute where he had lived and worked for thirty years.

In 1820 William Dick, by delivering a course of lectures on veterinary science in the Freemason's Hall, Niddry Street, planted the seed which in later years has become The Royal Dick Veterinary College. Moving in 1833 into new purpose built premises, for whose erection he himself provided almost the entire £2,500 which they cost. Dick was able to provide not only more comfortable accommodation for the increasing number of students from home and overseas but also better facilities for teaching and especially for practical demonstrations. Situated in Clyde Street and built around a rectangular courtyard the new college had a dissecting room, accommodation for sick animals, a lecture room towards whose furnishing The Highland Society donated £50, and a chemical laboratory to which was added, over the archway entrance, living quarters for himself and his sister, Mary, who kept the college accounts and supervised the behaviour of the students. William Dick died in 1866 and by his Will bequeathed the college, along with a considerable endowment, in trust to the Lord Provost and the magistrates of Edinburgh, who now became responsible for the management of its affairs (Note 9). That there should be teething troubles was to be anticipated. A new office of Principal of the College was introduced and in the short space of two years there were two holders of the office - Professors Hallen and Williams. In the autumn of 1869 two new professors joined the staff, Branford to teach anatomy and Dewar to teach chemistry. Before taking up his duties, James Dewar had several improvements made to the chemistry laboratory which he described as "being deficient in many respects". The account was £44 14s. 10d. and when it was queried by some of the trustees he wrote in reply that he was absolutely convinced that what had been done would be to the benefit of the students, adding in his forthright manner, "It seems ridiculous for anyone possessed of average knowledge to imagine that getting a table along with gas and water could have nothing to do with analysis or investigation". The twenty-seven-year-old professor knew his mind and was not going to be trifled with. The appointment of Branford to the chair of anatomy was an unmitigated disaster. Quite early in the session the senior students detected how deficient was his knowledge of the subject. Not only did he make many mistakes indeed howlers, in his lectures, but he was also incompetent in the dissecting room, where his attendance was much less frequent than it was supposed to be. Sometimes his lecture, which ought to have lasted an hour, was over in thirty minutes and on occasion it was read verbatim from printed books to which the students had access. When questions were put to him he had often to consult a manual in order to obtain the answer. The upshot was that his dissatisfied students presented a petition to the authorities demanding his removal and when this was not forthcoming they resorted to disruptive tactics in the lecture room; stamping their feet, singing, kicking the boards in front of their benches and even shooting swan shot at the lecturer. Professor Dewar's laboratory boy picked up several pipes and a lot of shot from the floor of Branford's lecture room. As Secretary of the college young Professor Dewar was drawn into the dispute. Student insubordination, like all hooliganism, is never completely self- contained. There is an overspill which affects the innocent. Of the students who attended his lectures Professor Dewar said that until after Christmas, when their opposition to Branford became vehement, "they behaved extremely well and paid attention to the lectures, so much so, that I said to them" - with a touch of humour, one imagines - "that I was agreeably disappointed at their conduct." After Christmas he did have one spot of bother. It was his custom, as he had agreed with the students, to appear on the lecture platform seven minutes after the appointed hour, when he expected them all to be in the room and seated. During the weeks of unsettlement in the college when he passed in through the gateway he often found them standing at the en- trance, "listening to a hurdy gurdy or organ grinder or a bagpipe player", which he told them was quite ungentlemanly conduct. One day some students were very late having been engaged, as one of them confessed, "in kicking an old hat about in Clyde Street'. When the latecomers reached the classroom door they found that the professor had locked it and had commenced his lecture. The outsiders had indulged in noise and shouting hoping thereby, but unsuccessfully as it turned out, to cause the lecturer to cease. Next day when Professor Dewar arrived he found that he was locked; so he went back to the laboratory and resumed his work there. On the next day, when things had returned to normal, he reprimanded them sternly for their misconduct and one student had the decency to apologise which "I regarded as a gentlemanly thing to do". Young though he was, James Dewar was a firm disciplinarian who regarded it as his duty to rebuke in the plainest terms any misbehaviour inside or outside the college. "When I heard them swearing in St Andrew's Square as I passed along or saw them drunk standing in the college yard I interfered, as I felt I was morally bound to do as a professor." He was quite sure, and experience proved him right, that firm dealing with miscreants earned the proper response and that to treat serious misbehaviour as a joke was only to invite worse misconduct. Possessing a thorough mastery of his subject James Dewar was an effective teacher. One of his pupils, an elderly gentleman still alive in 1923, remembered his late teacher "as brimful of energy and enthusiasm which he communicated to his class". As Principal Williams said, "Professor Dewar is a first rate chemist and when he tones down, with a little more experience, he will be a first rate teacher." But it was to research that he was devoted heart and soul, working in the chemical laboratory until usually one or two o'clock in the morning.

In his autobiography John Gray McKenrick, later to become Professor of Physiology in Glasgow University, tells how, when he was one day in the office of the Principal of the Veterinary College, a young man entered and "introducing himself he said, 'you and I should know each other Dr McKenrick'. The young man was James Dewar whose scientific contributions to The Royal Society of Edinburgh I had read. That introduction not only influenced my future career but produced a warm personal friendship that will last till the end of our lives." A few days later they met again in the quadrangle of the university and Dewar suggested that together they should begin researches on the effect of light on the eye. This led not only to an academically fruitful partnership between the chemist and the physiologist but to the important discovery that when light falls on the living retina an electrical current is produced which can be recognised with a sensitive galvanometer. Dr McKenrick provides an interesting account of the weeks and months of eager experimentation which resulted in their joint authorship of four papers read in 1874 to the Royal Society of Edinburgh. "I shall never forget" he writes "the evening when, in a little room upstairs above the chemical laboratory in Clyde Street we made the discovery by noticing a movement of the spot of light on the scale of the galvanometer when the light of a taper fell on the isolated eyeball of a frog. This led to a prolonged investigation which attracted the attention of scientific men in Edinburgh and London and elsewhere. Without our knowledge and about the same time a similar discovery had been made by Holmgren, a physiologist in Upsala. As the investigation had to be conducted in the dark and quiet hours, the time we worked was during the night. Dewar usually came

107

to my house in Castle Terrace soon after 10pm and we then went to the laboratory and worked till two or even three in the morning. This went on for many weeks. In these midnight vigils we were frequently accompanied by friends who came to witness the experiments. On one occasion we had the company of Thomas Huxley who was spending the winter in Edinburgh in charge of the Natural History class during the absence of Wyville Thomson as Director of The Challenger Expedition. Probably the night watchman often wondered what was going on in the laboratory in the hours of early morning - the 'wee short 'oor ayont the twal'. On one occasion one clear night we took part of the apparatus into the street, the galvanometer being in the little room above the laboratory. We had a frog's eye staring at the full moon, to the light of which there was an electrical response. Our joint researches were such as could be most efficiently carried out by a combination of a physicist with a physiologist. In a way it marked an epoch in the lives of both of us. Our investigations followed more of a chemical and physiological nature; Dewar made the chemical substance to be examined and I tested it on animal life. In particular, we examined the physiological action of chinaline and pyridene bases and we laid the foundation which led to the invention by the Germans of not a few artificial chemical compounds, now used in medicine, such as antipyrin, etc. Following the researches of Thomas Fraser and Crum Brown we were on the lines of establishing a relation between chemical composition and physiological action, a view now of great importance in medicine." Dewar and McKendrick made the results of these novel and interesting experiments known to a wider public by the papers which they communicated to The Royal Society of

Edinburgh (Note 10). On 21st April 1873 they submitted the first of four instalments on "The Physiological Action of Light". As these papers provide the earliest example of the pattern which Dewar followed in all his researches an analysis of their content is not without interest and value to the student of his many varied activities. The opening paragraphs reveal a wide knowledge of what had been written by earlier thinkers on the topic under consideration and indicated what he considered to be the flaws in their arguments. "Numerous hypotheses have been made by physicists and physiologists but up to the present date our knowledge of the subject is without any experimental foundation." Then the several hypotheses by Newton, Vielloni, Seebeck, Young, Du Bois-Reynaud, Draper and Mosier are quoted, none of which had been supported by experiment. Having exposed this deficiency he concludes that there is "obvious need for careful and refined experiment" and in this the two young scientists saw an uncultivated field for research. Their enquiry is to be in two parts, "(1) to ascertain the electro motive force of the retina and (optic) nerve and (2) to observe whether this was altered in amount by the action of light". Using the method devised by Du Bois-Reynaud they had no difficulty in obtaining a strong deflection from the eyes of various rabbits, a cat, a dog, a pigeon, a tortoise, numerous frogs and a goldfish. "The deflection was often so much as to drive the spot of light off the galvanometer scale. In regard to (2) they found Du Bois-Reynaud's galvanometer inadequate so they used Sir William Thomson's "exceedingly sensitive reflecting galvanometer kindly lent to us by Professor Tait". Difficulties, such as the dying of the nerve had to be overcome but the experimenters succeeded in this and they record that "up to this date about five hundred observations were made . . . and we took every occasion to obtain accurate results". As always with Dewar nothing was left to chance. No pains were spared in the thoroughness with which research was planned, the carefulness with which preparations were made and the meticulous care with which the observations were made and recorded before conclusions were drawn. In this case, his conclusions with his usual love of clarity are recorded in nine paragraphs. (1) The action of light on the retina is to alter the amount of the electro- motive force to the extent of from three to seven per cent of the total amount of the natural current. (2) A flash of light lasting a fraction of a second produces a marked effect. (3) A lighted match held at a distance of four or five feet is sufficient to produce an effect. (4) The light of a small gas flame enclosed in a lantern and cased to pass through a globular glass jar (12 inches in diameter) filled with a solution of ammoniacal sulphate of copper or biocromath of potash has also produced a change in the amount of the electro-motive power. (5) The action of light on the eye of the frog is as follows: when a diffuse light is allowed to impinge on the eye of the frog, after it has arrived at a tolerably stable condition, the natural electro-motive power is in the first place increased; then diminished; during the continuation of light it is still slowly diminished to a point where it remains constant: and on the removal of light, there is a sudden increase of the electro-motive power nearly up to its original position. The alterations above referred to are variables, depending on the quality and intensity of the light employed, the position of the eyeball on the cushions and modifications in the vitality of the tissues. (6) Similar experiments with the eye of warm-blooded animals placed on the cushions as rapidly as possible after the death of the animal, and under the same conditions, have never given us an initial positive variation as we have above detailed in the case of the frog but always a negative variation. The after indirective effect on the withdrawal of light occurs in the same way. (7) Many experiments have been made as to the effect of light from different positions of the spectrum. . . . All these observations tend to show that the greatest effect is produced by those parts of the spectrum that appear to consciousness to be the most luminous, namely the yellow and green. (8) Similarly, experiments were made with light of varying intensity and show that the physical effects we have observed vary in such a manner as to correspond closely with the values that would result if the well-known law of Fechner was approximately true. (9) The method followed in these enquiries is a new method in physiological research and by the employment of proper appliances, it may be greatly extended not only with regard to vision but also to the other senses. In the last paragraph the experimenters are - characteristically of James Dewar - mapping out more virgin land to plough or, to change the metaphor, fresh worlds to conquer. In a progress report given on 5th May 1873, they recorded several improvements in method which they had made and which they followed up with a series of ten tabulated results three of which deserve mention - "(1) We have proved, using a frog, that the pigment cells of the skin in the vicinity of the cornea have nothing to do with the results obtained." (2) As to the effects produced by lights of different intensities; "If a candle is placed at a distance of one foot from the eye, and then is removed ten feet, the amount of light received by the eye is exactly one hundredth part of what it got at a distance of one foot, whereas the electromagnetic

111

force, instead of being altered in the same proportion, is reduced by one third. (3) It was apparent to us that these experiments would ultimately bear upon the theory of sense perception as connected with vision." Again on 2nd July, they reported on their experiments carried out by moonlight with the following results; "(1) The light from a beam of uncondensed moonlight, though of weak intensity and almost entirely free from heat rays is still sufficient to alter the electro motive power of the nerve and retina. (2) We have examined the phenomenon in the eyes of the following animals: the common newt, the goldfish, the rockling, the stickleback, the common edible crab, the lobster. The eye of the goldfish and rockling, both sluggish fishes, were found to resemble each other inasmuch as the vibrations in the electro motive force were slow - a marked contrast to those of the active and alert stickleback the eye of which was very sensitive to light. The experiments on the eyes of crustacea are of importance because they show that the action of light on the compound eye is the same as on the simple eye. (3) The action of light on the electro motive force of the living eye in cats and birds - pigeon and owl - has been observed by putting the cat or bird under the influence of chloroform. The eye of a snake was examined and its action resembled that of the frog. (4) Now we can state that the law of the variation in the electro motive force of the retina and optic nerve holds good in the following groups of the animal kingdom: - mammalia - aves - reptilla - amphibia - pisces and crustacea." With boldness - but with a legitimate boldness - they go on to say that the law of Fechner is not "as has been hitherto supposed a function of the brain alone but is really a function of the terminal organ - the retina". A further brief paper concluded their account of their physiological enquiries. A few months later the duo sent in a paper. "On the physiological action of ozone" - 1st December 1873. This also was, they noted, a hitherto unexplored area for investigation. After detailing a method for producing ozone they recounted how they watched "the action of ozone on the living animal imprisoned in an atmosphere containing a large proportion of the gas and the action it exerted on the individual living tissues of the body." In these experiments they used frogs, birds, mice, rabbits - and ourselves!" Of the last instance they wrote, "On breathing an atmosphere of ozonised oxygen the chief effects observed were a suffocating feeling in the chest, a tendency to breathe slowly, an irritation of the back of the throat and of the glottis and a tingling sensation, referred to the skin of the face and conjunctivae. The pulse became feebler. After breathing it as long as it was judicious to do so, for five or eight minutes, the suffocating feeling became stronger and we were obliged to desist. The experiment was followed by violent, irritating cough and sneezing and for five or six hours thereafter by a sensation of rawness in the throat and air passages". They went on to detail the action of ozone on the circulation, the reflex action of the spinal cord, muscular contractibility, the blood, the ciliary motion. Among the conclusions they reached were these: the inhalation of an atmosphere highly charged with ozone exercises a destructive action on the living animal tissues if brought into immediate contact with them. On 2nd March 1874 along with Professor Guthrie Tait, James Dewar read a paper to the Royal Society of Edinburgh which is significant in that it indicates the shape of things to come so far as his fruitful interest in vacua goes. It was entitled "On a new method of obtaining very perfect vacua". After outlining the methods devised by earlier explorers in that field, such as Davy, Andrews and Gassiot they go on, "the method we have devised to absorb traces of gases is based on the remarkable power of absorption of cocoa nut charcoal for gaseous bodies generally. . . . We need hardly say that this easy method of obtaining vacua will be of importance in spectroscopic observations and we intend shortly to communicate observations in this direction". In a paper on cystine he concluded with this plea, "The author's stock of cystine being now exhausted he will feel extremely indebted to anyone who would spare him a small quantity for experimental purposes". An active member of the Society, of which he had been elected a councillor on 24th November 1873, James Dewar contributed more than twenty articles to their proceedings dealing with experiments which he had carried out alone or with colleagues during the short period of his membership; a remarkable output in quantity as it was also in originality for one so young and a harbinger of the amazing number of scientific papers which were to come from his pen in future years. By 1873 such was his established, and growing, reputation that he was invited to deliver a lecture at The Royal Institution in London for which he chose as his subject, "The temperature of the sun and the work of sunlight."

In 1870, his brother Alexander, now a doctor in Melrose (Note 11), sent him a sample of water for analysis taken from a well which had been dug recently and "whose water is perfectly different from all those in its vicinity". In his reply James wrote, "should it maintain its present character I have no doubt that, judging from its own qualities as well as from its favourable climatic situation along with the general interest attached to the locality this chalybeate is certain to recommend itself to the medical profession."

The Directors of the Highland and Agricultural Society of Scotland (Note 12), which had for many years been ably served by Dr Thomas Anderson as its chemist, resolved at their meeting on 8th January 1873 to engage an assistant chemist, who in addition to sharing Dr Anderson's analytical work; would "give lectures in different districts and superintend the carrying out of field experiments at a salary of £100 to £150 per annum". On 5th March they approved "the appointment of Mr James Dewar, F.R.S.E., who at present holds the professorship of chemistry at Edinburgh Veterinary College and is assistant to the professor of chemistry in the University". One advantage to the Society's East of Scotland members was that James Dewar was based in Edinburgh and so was more readily accessible to them than was Dr Anderson who was domiciled in Glasgow. Among the duties of the assistant chemist was to reply to letters craving advice and to analyse samples of manure sent to him by individual farmers. On 21st January 1874 Dr Anderson resigned owing to ill health and he concluded his half yearly report in these terms: "I shall leave it to Mr James Dewar, of whom I have a very high opinion to report on the work which he has done." During the previous six months James Dewar had received only five samples of manure for analysis and "during the whole of that period no application had been received from any agricultural association requesting lectures on the application of chemistry to agriculture or the execution of the field experiments proposed by the Society". This part of the

Directors' plan had fallen flat, much to the disappointment of the keen and innovative as well as outstandingly able young chemist whom they had chosen. Six months later he reported that the work of his department had increased and that he had found no grave adulteration of manures, as the supplying firms were now buying the ingredients and mixing them according to soil and crops (Note 13).

He added a note about training well educated young men "who might be induced by the quality of the instruction training they received to become, after some time, useful assistants in the discharge of the Society's work". True to form James Dewar was looking ahead and envisaging beneficial developments. At the General Meeting of the Society on 20th January 1875 he remarked that the number of requests for analyses of guanos, manures, feeding stuffs and other substances had exceeded that of any previous year. The farming community was beginning to realise the worth of the service he was offering. He had noticed no grave cases of adulteration but several samples of oilcake which contained "large proportions of nutritive substances were rendered dangerous and inferior from the presence of a large proportion of sand". As oilcake was sold by weight and as sand is heavy, farmers were being seriously cheated by some unscrupulous suppliers. Thorough in everything he did, James Dewar appended to the analysis what he considered to be the real value of the product, manure or oilcake, which had been sent to him in order that his clients could appreciate the margin by which they were swindled by the supplier. Not content with examining only the samples of guano sent to him James Dewar obtained others from Berry Barclay and Co. of Leith, one of the principal importers of Peruvian guano. This raw guano was found to be of good quality and of the dissolved guano, he wrote, "it continues to contain the amount of ammonia and phosphates guaranteed by Ohlendorf and Co. who hold the special con- cession of manufacture from the Peruvian Government". This comment indicated clearly to farmers a reliable source from which they could obtain good quality guano - a very useful service indeed! In scientific investigation he was ever ready to go the second mile. He was always looking for uncultivated fields which he could till for the benefit of the community he served. In his role as chemist to those who were almost wholly dependent on wells for potable water, he began to analyse the water used for domestic purposes by some members of the Society. He found that it was often "contaminated with sewage matter generating on exposure to light numerous infusoria. Confirmation of the unhealthy state of people using such waters has been derived from their medical attendant and the attention of all members of the Society ought to be directed to the danger of using waters in any way liable to get surface or sewage drainage, as often occurs in wells sunk near farms". This report, issued nationwide to the members of the Agricultural Society, alerted the farming community to the urgent need to examine the location of the sources of potable water and to the advisability of stinking deep wells at appropriate places.

In April 1875 the Secretary of the Society received from James Dewar a letter addressed from St Peter's College, Cambridge, submitting his resignation as assistant chemist in consequence of his having been elected to the Jacksonian Chair of Chemistry in the University of Cambridge. In his letter he indicated that he had "intended prosecuting investigations in vegetable physiology". Ever an investigator, had he remained in the employment of the Society he would not have confined his energies to analysis but would have broadened his activities, as a real agricultural chemist should, by relating the knowledge he gained through research to every aspect of farming and thus leading the farmers, whom he was engaged to serve, on towards maximising both quality and output from the soil. In his letter he could not refrain from talking a swipe at the dullards on the committee who failed to understand the difference between a mere analyser and an agricultural chemist (Note 14). In accepting his resignation the Directors of the Society adopted unanimously the following resolution: "The Directors cannot accept Professor Dewar's resignation of the office of assistant chemist without recording in their minutes their sense of the value of his services and their regret at the loss to the Society of such a distinguished chemist. At the same time they congratulated him on having been appointed to such an honourable position." At the Society's general meeting on 16th June 1875, the final report by Professor Dewar referred to the steadily increasing work load which he had had. "During the past three weeks alone I have analysed twenty samples of manures and feeding stuffs". Only one serious instance of adulteration had come to his notice. A sample of penguin guano contained 32% sand and clay. The market price was £10 per ton and he estimated the worth of the sample to be about £5 per ton. One case of suspected poisoning had occurred recently and the stomach was found to contain lead. There is a nigger in every wood pile and at this meeting it was in the form of a 'gentleman' farmer, Milne Home from

Wedderburn, who complained that "Dr Anderson had got into bad health and for two years drew his salary without doing anything for the Society and his assistant, Mr Dewar, had told them that he was not so much an agricultural as a scientific chemist. . . . They had therefore been paying for two years £1,000 to these two gentlemen and they had not had a bit of work done for the benefit of the Society." When Mr Dewar asked leave to reply to these stupid remarks, as he no doubt would have done most effectively, for he had a sharp tongue, the chairman ruled that it would be out of order - and the 'gentleman farmer' should have been grateful! At the next meeting on January 19th 1876, with Dr Anderson now dead and Professor Dewar safely away in Cambridge the 'gentleman farmer', now uninhibited, returned to his abuse of these two loyal and distinguished servants of the Society. One, however, cannot leave this phase of James Dewar's career without the comment that had he continued as chemist to The Highland Society and been given the unstinted support of its members, which his ability and enthusiasm undoubtedly merited, he would have become the most distinguished chemist in its history whose work as a pioneer of good husbandry, in all its aspects, would have been of inestimable benefit to Scottish farming. But it was not to be. His departure for Cambridge and eventually London was, if to Scottish farming a great loss, an immense gain to other branches of chemical research and for himself the first step on the road which was to lead to an international reputation and enduring fame.

Engrossed as he was to be all his life in chemistry as a teacher and researcher James Dewar did not neglect the humanities.

Sir James Crichton Brown who knew him intimately spoke of him as "being deeply read in general literature and a great lover of poetry as he was of her sister music, as well as a connoisseur of painting and objets d'art". We may be sure that these cultural interests were not neglected during his busy youthful years in Edinburgh and that the strains of the Tulliallan fiddle would be often heard in his lodgings. In his Edinburgh years he was also a frequenter of the theatre, as a witness a letter which he wrote to Lady Martin on 25th February 1893 in which, after thanking her for a copy of her book, he says, "I regard the gift as a very great honour. The personal interest to me is beyond all expression, seeing that your embodiment of Shakespeare's heroines were the means of instilling into my youthful mind love and appreciation of truth and beauty. Without this spiritual impulse life would have indeed been poorer".

He and his brother, Alexander, were members of Bristo United Presbyterian Church whose junior minister, the Rev. Thomas Dunlop, inducted on 13th June 1871, assisted at his marriage. The intimation of the event in The Scotsman is as follows: "At 19 Grange Loan on the 8th August 1871, by the Rev. Dr Wallace, Old Greyfriars, assisted by the Rev. Thomas Dunlop, Bristo United Presbyterian Church, James Dewar F.R.S.E. to Helen Ross, eldest surviving daughter of the late William Banks, Engraver and Printer, Edinburgh". Theirs was to prove a singularly happy marriage, as those who knew them longest and most intimately, were to testify on the occasion of their golden wedding celebrations. "His wife's influence over him was absolute," wrote Professor Armstrong,

'and his devotion to her was increasing and measureless."
(Note 15)

During his Edinburgh years James Dewar became known to an increasingly wide circle of scientists through his articles in Nature and his participation in the proceedings of the British Association for the Advancement of Science. At their meetings in Liverpool in 1870 he communicated two papers to the Chemical Section, entitled Notes on Thermal Equivalents: a) Fermentation and b) Oxide of Chlorine. This was followed in June 1871 with a report on "The Thermal Equivalents of the Oxides of Chlorine". The results, he said, were merely preliminary and he demonstrated "in a remarkable manner the difficulties attending this class of investigation". Two months later the British Association awarded him a grant of £15 to enable him to continue his studies. In November 1872 he was delivering Friday evening lectures at the Royal Institution in London and in 1873 he contributed to Nature an article dealing with "Recent Researches on the Physiological Action of Light" and in collaboration with his friend Dr McKenrick a paper entitled "Physiological Action of Ozone". In March 1873 we find him lecturing to the Chemical Society on "Dissociation" and at The British Association for Advancement of Science on "Latent Heat of Liquified Gases", the author, we are told, having "deduced a formula for calculating the latent heat of a gas from the known tension of that gas", the results of his investigation having already been communicated to the Chemical Section of which his friend and colleague, Professor Crum Brown, was that year's chairman. Thus the name of James Dewar had become, very early in his career, familiar in the world of science and his reputation as a careful investigator and a pioneer in several fields of enquiry was being established. Early in 1875 Robert Willis the Jacksonian Professor of Natural and Experimental Philosophy at Cambridge University died. His salary had been £300 per annum which the Senate decided to raise to £500 for his successor who was to be obliged "to reside in the precincts of the University for eighteen weeks in every academical year and give no fewer than forty lectures in every academic year". There were five applicants for the office: Rev. J.

C. Ellis, who had been Professor Willis's deputy for two years; James Stuart, a Fellow of Trinity College; Professor H.E. Arm- strong of the London Institution; W. N. Hartly, Demonstrator of Chemistry in King's College and E, J. Mills, D.Sc., Examiner in Chemistry at London University - all eminent men. But when it became known that James Dewar was being considered they all withdrew. Though not an applicant he was appointed, in April, after an interview and on the strong recommendation of Professors T. Guthrie Tait and Humphrey. The Senate's choice evoked universal approval. The contingent in Nature is typical: "As our readers know, Mr Dewar has already done excellent work and is so widely known as a gifted investigator as well as a first rate teacher that his presence at Cambridge will be a great gain not only to that university but to English science." A strange and unusual condition was attached to the tenure of the Jackonian Chair. By the will of the founder, the professor was charged "to have an eye more particularly to that opprobrium medicorum - the gout". The new holder of the office took this request seriously and carried out a number of experiments, some of which were on himself, with a view to discovering a cure for the malady. " But, "as his friend Henry Armstrong informs us, "the only outcome unfortunately was that he spoiled his own digestion and so, in later years, he had to become an extraordinary careful liver". The thirty-four-year-old professor took up his duties in January 1876 and the subject of his first course of lectures was "Organic and Animal Chemistry". In the following year, out of a total of fifty-seven candidates for the Fellowship of the Royal Society - F.R.S. - who had offered themselves for election, James Dewar was one of the successful fifteen. In the circumscribed but enthusiastic and hospitable society of Edinburgh the young professor had co-operated eagerly with some of the leading scientists in Britain both in research at the university and in discussions at meetings of The Royal Society of Edinburgh. He found the atmosphere in Cambridge less congenial. Cambridge University had been devoted to the humanities for centuries. Conditions for scientific research were primitive. The authorities were as yet reluctant to equate the physical sciences with the other entrenched subjects in the curriculum. James Dewar found that he had to work in a small room in a two-storied building. But there were compensations. He had Clerk Maxwell for a colleague and Professor George Liveing who, though much his senior in age, offered him warm friendship and together, over a period of twenty years, they conducted a large number of experiments in spectroscopy, the results of which were communicated to the world of science in seventy-eight papers in a volume entitled Collected Papers in Spectroscopy by George Liveing and James Dewar. Of his skill as a lecturer The Scottish Leader had this to say: "Professor Dewar is one of the clearest and most interesting lecturers of the day and delivers the most elaborate and difficult discourses without the assistance of even the briefest notes." Fortunate indeed were the students who had such an instructor.

Two years after coming to Cambridge he was chosen to be the Fullerian Professor of Chemistry at The Royal Institution, London (Note 16). Prior to his appointment he had delivered two Friday evening lectures at The Royal Institution in which he described the work which he and Dr J. G. McKenrick had done on the effect of light on the retina and optic nerve. The latter of the two lectures, says a distinguished scientist who was present, was "a remarkable tour de force exhibiting the facility of experimental resource and brilliance of demonstration which have been ever characteristic of Professor Dewar's lectures and rendered them so peculiarly attractive and instructive". His ability to communicate easily and lucidly not only with his compeers but with those less well versed in scientific matters allied to his brilliance as an experimental chemist fitted him admirably for the duties of his new appointment (Note 17). He retained both chairs, spending part of the academic year in Cambridge and part in London. But it was to The Royal Institution that he devoted the lion's share of his time and it was there that he carried out the experiments which brought him world-wide fame. Working conditions at The Royal Institution were vastly superior to the cramped accommodation in Cambridge and when through the munificence of Dr Ludwig Mond, who purchased the adjoining house, No. 20 Albemarle Street, and had it altered to form the Davy-Faraday Laboratory James Dewar, who was appointed its first Director, was provided with superb facilities and ample scope for the exercise of his talents. The new laboratory was opened by The Prince of Wales on 22nd December 1896. Dr Ludwig Mond who was a close and admiring friend of Dewar provided also a lift to the Director's flat to which he himself was a frequent visitor. In 1887 James Dewar had been appointed Superintendent of the House and took up residence on the top floor in the rooms which had been occupied by Faraday,

> "Great Faraday, who made the world so wise
> And loved the labour better than the wage."

To a man of Dewar's sensitivity and who held Faraday in great reverence it must have been a thrilling and inspiring experience to have become the occupant of what was once Faraday's home. With a connoisseur's love of beauty he and his wife furnished their flat with fine tapestries, lovely Persian carpets, attractive paintings and engravings to which were being constantly added many objets d'art all of which reflected their exquisite taste. Here for thirty years they had their home which was a centre of generous hospitality to their large circle of friends and a salon where men of science and lovers of literature and the arts were always made welcome. As Superintendent of The Royal Institution he was responsible for directing and advising on research. Of a generous disposition, he was always ready to assist his colleagues and students, though he could be brusquely intolerant of shoddy work which he sometimes "damned with not too faint praise". If he had any fault it lay in his irascibility to which he occasionally gave expression too plainly and which was not helped by his proneness to insomnia. As is the case with most great men James Dewar was extremely modest. As a colleague remarked, "he was a man of incorrigible modesty". He never boasted of his achievements or rated his attainments highly and was anxious that others should not do so. "Every morning," we are told by one of his assistants, "James Dewar appeared in the laboratory at 10.30 prompt and kept his finger on all that happened day by day. He had a habit of humming more or less tunefully as he went about the building which gave the staff ample warning of his approach. Methodical in everything he did, he drew up a detailed code of rules for the guidance of those whom he called his working staff which all had to sign." Though an exacting master he had a magnetic personality and, says Ralph Cory, who served him for twenty-five years, and who became eventually the librarian of The Royal Institution, "there was something about him that far outweighed his occasional petulant outbursts and won the unqualified loyalty of his sub-ordinates. When he was knighted I was given a crisp £5 note, enormous largesse in these days, with which to celebrate the honour in a fitting manner" (Note 18). His principal assistant in the laboratory was a 'brither Scot', Robert Lennox and junior to him was Mr Heath, each of whom tragically lost an eye as the result of explosions during experiments at The Royal Institution. James Dewar's work there was marked by amazing productivity not in one department of scientific research alone but in several. Few scientists have equalled him either in the volume or in the wide ranging variety of his investigations.

The Royal Institution, founded by Count Rumford in 1799, was one of the earliest scientific research centres in Great Britain. As its Charter makes clear, although it was meant to encourage research it was also intended to be a vehicle for communicating these results to the general public. This dual aim has continued to be its principal objective throughout its long history. To discharge the latter purpose two parallel courses of lectures have been organised each year – the Friday night lectures geared to the small group of professional, well informed scientists whose advanced knowledge enabled them to understand the niceties of the current advances in research; and a series of popular lectures pitched in a key more suitable to the requirements of the intelligentsia who had the layman's interest in science. The average number of Friday evening lectures ran to about twenty per annum and the number of popular lectures was considerably more. There was also a series of Christmas lectures inaugurated by Faraday for senior school children who had a special interest in science. Besides having to arrange for the participation of suitable lecturers for each series James Dewar undertook a generous share in lecturing. Referring to this in 1921, on the occasion of the professor's golden wedding, the President of The Royal Institution, The Duke of Northumberland, said: "In the last forty-four years he has delivered more than fifty Friday evening lectures, thirty-six sets of lectures covering the whole range of chemistry and chemico-physics, nine sets of Christmas lectures to juveniles firmly establishing in the minds of the rising generation a foundation of scientific study." His lectures were eagerly awaited and they always ensured a full house, the audience being attracted not only by the substance of the lecture itself but even more by the truly astonishing experiments he made during its course. Each lecture, to which he gave intense thought, was a meticulously prepared work of art. He took immense pains with his experiments to ensure that every detail was right. Nothing was ever left to chance. His lecture was like a Paris model sometimes appearing very simple but let anyone less skilful try to copy it and he would quickly find himself in trouble. Like Turner, James Dewar 'painted' for the sheer joy of doing it. "He set a standard" says Professor Armstrong, "which made The Royal Institution lectures famous, especially on account of his daring experiments. I can never forget the impression I received when I first saw him burn diamond under liquid air – the gradual accretion of the carbon dioxide snow shower and the blueing of the fluid by ozone, also demonstrated by the iodine test: then the rapid uprush of the mercury in a barometer tube full of air when the tube was cooled by liquid hydrogen: it all but knocked the top off: or again the production of ozone at the surface of solid oxygen by the impact of ultra violet radiations. At such moments – and there were many such – the heart beat with joy at the significance of his feats of inspiration." Such was the impact of one of James Dewar's Friday evening lectures on an eminent contemporary man of science. Professor McKendrick, who, on several occasions, lectured at the Friday sessions during his tenure of the Chair of Physiology in Glasgow University has this to say about them: "They were for men who had done original work on their subject which they brought before the audience. The lecture hour was nine to ten p.m. and punctuality at both ends was a firm condition. On the stroke of the hour – after a time for conversazione – the Director and Lecturer who took his place at the horse shoe table where Faraday and other great men have stood, entered. The chairman made no remarks by way of introduction or vote of thanks. And before the stroke of the bell in the entrance hall I felt like the man who had taken his place on the drop." The lecture concluded, the lecturer and others adjourned to enjoy the generous hospitality of the lady of the house and to continue their learned discussion in the comfort of the Director's flat. Ralph Cory who was in the service of The Royal Institution for fifty years recalls an amusing incident, of which there were few at the Friday evening lectures. In 1904 Korea was much in the news. On one occasion the lecture was given by a distinguished ecclesiastical dignitary The Rt. Hon. And Rt. Rev. the Count Vay de Vaya and Luskod who created a sensation by appearing in all the splendour of his gorgeous Episcopal robes of scarlet and purple. "I can still remember," writes Cory, "Dewar's face when he first beheld the vision splendid and for once – and once only – James Dewar was at a loss for words." In the other lectures the net was cast to attract a wider audience. They were intended for the intelligent layman and such was the skill of the guest lecturers and of James Dewar himself that abstruse subjects were expounded, by the spoken word and appropriate illustrations, in such a manner that those whose knowledge of science was little more than rudimentary could understand in general terms the import of the lecture. The result was that these lectures always commanded a full house. Only very rarely did the good seed fall on such poor soil as that of the mind of a lady who reported that the lecture she attended was about maggots and that the lecturer showed creepy crawly things on a sheet. For maggots read magnets and for creeping things read shadows of iron filings! In most

129

cases the audience came away considerably enlightened and, like Oliver Twist, asking for more and some there were in whom was kindled the desire to undertake serous study. Not every man of great scholarship can adapt himself and his learning to the juvenile mind. But once again the versatility of James Dewar and the lecturers associated with him is vindicated. The titles of the lectures which he himself gave were such as to arouse the curiosity of intelligent youth, as the following half dozen culled at random from a very large number will show: Atoms – Alchemy related to modern science – The story of a meteorite, with experimental illustrations – Frost and Fire – Clouds and Cloudland – Air, gaseous and liquid. James Dewar had for long been interested in photography not only as forming a means of investigation but as a method of permanently recording observations which could be studied at leisure and had made use of it in the research which he conducted with Professor Liveing. To young people, who were becoming increasingly interested in photography – and there were many such – his lectures in 1888 when his subject was, The chemistry of light and photography, must have been particularly interesting. Arrangements were made for the introduction of a powerful beam of electric light equal in intensity to a sunbeam, into the theatre for the photographic experiments he was to make. If the juvenile audience were interested in what he had to say they were invariably enthralled as they watched the magician wave his magic wand in the experiments which accompanied the spoken word. Other lecturers sometimes resorted to more flamboyant means to interest their audience. Once a theatrical production was staged in which a group of children carefully chosen and trained illustrated the discovery of the planet

Neptune by de Berrier. On another occasion, Professor James Kendall, speaking about young chemists and great discoveries, delivered his lecture on Faraday dressed up to impersonate the celebrated scientist. On still another occasion the lecturer brought in a young pet jaguar who was given a dish of milk on the lecture table, which he lapped up very quietly, in marked contrast to the growls and snarls with which he tackled a piece of raw meat, illustrating how the taste of blood aroused his more savage instincts. The same lecturer, on another occasion, introduced a lion cub which allowed himself to be petted. The lecturers in their turn were frequently surprised – and very pleasantly so – by the intelligent questions asked by members of their youthful audience and the knowledge which lay behind these questions. Sir Ambrose Fleming, who was a frequent and popular speaker on these occasions (Note 19), often recalled a conversation which he overheard between a father and his schoolboy son. As they retired, the gentleman said to his small son – "I heard everything the lecturer said but I must confess I did not understand all of it." To which they boy replied – "Never mind, dad, I understood it all right, and when we get home I'll explain it to you."

In November 1889 James Dewar who was as ardent a student of the history of chemistry as he was of the science in general be- came one of the founder members of The Gilbert Club whose aim was to do justice to the memory of William Gilbert, President of the Royal College of Physicians and who, when Francis Bacon was talking about the experimental method of scientific enquiry had begun it and was practising it. In 1600 Gilbert published his De Magnete which marks the starting point of the science of electricity and magnetism. Gilbert, who was born in Colchester and is buried in Holy Trinity Church, may well be regarded as the father of these two subjects. The purpose of the Gilbert Club was to perpetuate his memory, arrange for an English translation of his seminal work, De Magnete and plan for a suitable celebration of the tercentenary in 1900 of its publication.

High piled books in charactry would be needed even to catalogue the products of Professor Dewar's teeming brain far less discuss them. Thanks to the diligence of Lady Dewar, assisted by a few scientific friends, a small harvest has been gleaned and preserved from the multitude of his papers. Within the scope of a brief record of his life and work it is possible to mention only high points in his busy and crowded career of research and lecturing as a scientist.

Although in the eighteenth century Lavoisier remarked that if the earth were removed to very cold regions such as those of Jupiter or Saturn it atmosphere, or at least a part of it, would re- turn to a liquid condition; the history of the liquefaction of gases does not begin until the following century. John Dalton in one of his essays in 1801 surmised that at a sufficiently low temperature all gases could be reduced to liquids. But it was not until 1823 that, at the instigation of Michael Faraday, Sir Humphrey Davy put that theory to the test of experiment, with some success. He failed with the three gases – oxygen, nitrogen and hydrogen. The first breakthrough was made by Cailletet and Pictet, who, though working independently, obtained a 'dynamic' through not a 'static' liquid as, say, the steam from a kettle bears to a cup of water. Other scientists, notably Wroblewski and Olszewski in Cracow, continued experiments in the liquefaction of oxygen and 1883 Olszewski announced to the French Academy that he had obtained oxygen in a completely liquid state, and that a few days later he had seen nitrogen as a liquid but that it had disappeared in a few seconds (Note 20). James Dewar who always kept himself informed as to the work of leading scientists at home and overseas gave, shortly thereafter, a fascinating lecture at The Royal Institution using the apparatus of Cailletet and Pictet. Here were new worlds for him to conquer and like Wilfred Thesiger the traveller "he always felt a compulsion to go where others have not been". No doubt he was inspired also by the thought that his predecessors Faraday and Davy had been two of the earliest experimentalists in the liquefaction of gases. James Dewar took up the work which had fallen from their hands and working in hyper-arctic regions he pioneered a path where never foot of man had trod. With the same heroic courage and dogged determination as Scott, Amundsen and Shackleton had shown in their explorations he pursued his investigations as he continued his journey towards the absolute zero – K degrees, which was his South Pole. In pursuit of his goal he turned the chemical laboratory in The Royal Institution into a virtual machine shop. True to form he sensed a further fresh field of enquiry waiting to be investigated, viz. the properties of matter under hitherto unattainable conditions of cold which the liquefaction of gases had rendered possible. The next period in his career may be called The Low Temperature Years, for the liquefaction of gas now became his chief, though by no means his only, concern. His interest in this subject goes back to the very early 1870s. In 1874 he read to The British Association for the Advancement of Science a paper on The Latent Heat of Liquid Gases the author having deduced a formula for calculating the latent heat of a gas from the known tension of that gas. In 1878, using Cailletet's apparatus he demonstrated, for the first time in Britain, the liquefaction of oxygen at one of The Royal Institution's Friday evening lectures and six years later on a similar occasion he notched up another first, by showing on an apparatus which he had constructed for optical projection the liquefaction of oxygen so that, to their delighted wonder, the audience could watch the process taking place. Later he devised and constructed a machine, weighing over two tons, from which liquefied oxygen could be drawn off in quantity by means of a valve to act as a cooling agent, by which time he was also producing liquid air at twenty litres per hour, occasioning the remark that Professor Dewar was supplying liquid air as if it were water.

On December 17th 1891 the President of the Royal Society at the commencement of their meeting, read to the Fellows a letter from Professor Dewar which had just come into his hand, stating that "at 3 p.m. that afternoon he had placed a quantity of liquid oxygen in the state of rapid ebullition in air (and therefore at a temperature of −181 Celsius) between the poles of the historic Faraday magnet in a cup-shaped piece of rock salt (which is not moistened by liquid oxygen, and therefore keeps it in the spheroidal state)" and to his surprise Professor Dewar saw the liquid oxygen, as soon as the magnet was stimulated, "suddenly leap up to the poles and remain there permanently attracted till it was evaporated". He was to show also that liquid ozone followed the same pattern of behaviour as the liquid oxygen had done. In 1897, working along with Henri Moisson the French scientist who had brought his apparatus to The Royal Institution, James Dewar liquefied fluorine which he was to succeed in solidifying in 1903. Together they also carried out a study of its properties in the liquid state. The boiling point of fluorine is –187 Celsius and there is no sign of solidification at –210 Celsius. A little of the liquid fluorine spilt accidentally set fire to the wooden floor.

By this time almost all the natural gases, apart from hydrogen, had been liquefied and it was in his long and arduous attempt to achieve that goal, in which he was often baffled but never defeated, that when spraying liquid air and oxygen with the hydrogen jet he found that in a few minutes the liquids congealed in hard solids "like snow" – and thus, for the first time solid oxygen was produced. Encouraged by this he continued his endeavours and on 10th May 1898 his long campaign was crowned with success. Hydrogen was liquefied. In the course of his research he had built at The Royal Institution a large refrigerating machine for the purpose. His achievement was welcomed with delight by scientists everywhere in the most laudatory terms, Moisson the French chemist called it "a wonder of modern chemistry". To James Dewar himself it must have brought a feeling of tremendous satisfaction akin to that of Tensing Sherpa and Edmund Hilary when they stood on the summit of Mount Everest (Note 21). As Sir William Ramsay, a distinguished contemporary scientist put it. "It is only those who have joined in serious attempts to solve the problems presented by Nature who can understand the exultation which fills the heart at the moment of success. Honours or rewards which may follow are not thought of". On 1st May 1899 Professor Dewar, when speaking about the work of The Royal Institution, said that having now obtained liquid hydrogen in considerable quantity he "had directly determined its temperature and other physical constants finding its boiling point to be much lower than previously supposed, namely 20 degrees above the zero of absolute temperature and attaining by exhaustion a temperature of only 15 degrees absolute". He added that pending the discovery of some lighter gas there was no way so far of being able to bridge the gap and reaching the zero point. Professor Dewar also took occasion to issue a warning against the exaggerated accounts of the properties of liquid air which, having originated in America, were now appearing in some popular magazines in Britain. Later in this same year by reaching a still lower temperature, 14 degrees absolute, he achieved the solidification of hydrogen when it appeared as "a clear ice like solid". It took some considerable further experimental work before liquid hydrogen could be obtained in quantity but by 1901 the obstacles had been overcome and on 13th June of that year five litres of liquid hydrogen were conveyed through the streets of London from Dewar's laboratory to the rooms of The Royal Society. Now, apart from the limiting condition of the expense involved, it was possible to produce any desired quantity of liquid hydrogen. With the solidification of hydrogen, achieved before the close of the century, it could be said that almost all the known gases were now reduced to liquid and solid form and in this remarkable scientific achievement James Dewar had played a notable part, having, after Moisson had obtained fluorine in the free state, working with Moisson had reduced it to liquid form in 1897. In 1868 Sir Norman Lockyer had suggested that the sun contained a hitherto unknown element which he called helium and which, in 1895, was found also to exist on the earth. This discovery was made by Sir William Ramsay. Helium, "a colour- less, odourless and tasteless gas" which was also the lightest of the inert gases was readily obtainable from hot springs. From those at Bath James Dewar obtained supplies but unfortunately they contained neon which froze and blocked the valves. This unfortunate occurrence coupled with the fact that James Dewar suffered a long spell of ill health from 1904 to 1906, resulted in the prize for being the first to solidify helium going to Professor Kammerlingh Onnes of Leyden University who employed a method suggested by James Dewar. On 5th March 1908 Onnes sent a telegram to the British scientist: "Converted helium into solid. Last evaporating parts show considerable vapour pressures as if liquid state is jumped over". Disappointed though he must have been at being prevented from adding yet another first to his list of successes in the liquefaction and solidification of gases James Dewar, with his customary generosity, telegraphed in reply: "Congratulations! Glad my anticipation of the possibility of the achievement by known methods confirmed. My helium work arrested by ill health but hope to continue later on". At their meetings that year he described to members of the British Association for the Advancement of Science the apparatus which Onnes had used and pointed out that what he himself had said to them in 1902 with respect to the liquefaction and the solidification of helium had been proved correct. James Dewar had obtained liquid helium boiling at 4.5 degrees absolute and a temperature of 3 degrees absolute had been reached without a sign of solidification. So he had been well on the way to success had circumstances not intervened to hinder him. Now that it was possible to liquefy nearly all the known gases the problem arose as to how they could be preserved in liquid form so that scientists might proceed to further investigation of their properties at liquid temperature and also undertake experiments researching the peculiarities of metals at very low temperatures. Until that problem was solved the labour which had been involved in the liquefaction of gases was of small avail. No scientist could come up with a solution. All were baffled. Dr Morris, who was with Professor Dewar in The Royal Institution at the time, tells how he used all kinds of contraptions to preserve liquid air or oxygen in quantities from day to day. Boxes containing powdered cork, hay or crumpled newspapers were used in vain attempts to reduce the evaporation of these cold liquids. On one occasion Dewar pressed Lady Dewar's hat box into service. But in spite of all his endeavours nothing was left of the cold liquid next morning. All had evaporated. Then, reflecting on his work with high vacua during his Edinburgh years (Note 22) and on the effectiveness of charcoal in absorbing gases and in particular on how coconut charcoal, if reduced to a very low temperature, was an effective agent for this purpose James Dewar by using a vacuum to jacket the glass vessel containing the cold liquid met with success. The distance between the walls needed to be only two or three millimetres with internal silvering of the vacuum space. Thus the sphinx-like riddle was solved. The use of low temperature charcoal made it possible to use metals such as brass, copper or nickel instead of glass for the construction of double jacketed vessels which contributed greatly to solving the problem of the safe storage and the transportation of liquid air and oxygen for, in the long run,

138

industrial and domestic uses. It was now Professor Onnes's turn to offer congratulations to James Dewar, which in the true spirit of science he did handsomely in a speech in 1904 when he spoke of "Dewar's magnificent invention, which may be called the most important appliance for operating at extremely low temperatures", adding that "the moment when a vacuum glass containing liquid oxygen was offered to the Prince of Wales at a meeting of The Royal Institution marks an era in low temperature research". For James Dewar the production of liquid gases was not an end in itself but a means to opening up further novel methods of research in which he was now to engage vigorously not only on his own but in collaboration with many other scientists in their specific fields of enquiry. Had he patented his invention of the vacuum flask James Dewar would have made an immense fortune but he was no Mr Worldly Wiseman in matters of finance. Like his great master, Faraday, "he loved the labour better than the wage" and it was left to a German firm to cash in on his great discovery and to develop and market that vacuum flask which, like the Waverley pen, "came as a boon and a blessing to men". At first, the small quantities of liquid gases which were available restricted his range of investigation, confining him to determining the properties of the liquids themselves but by the late nineties when these gases – air, oxygen and hydrogen – became more plentiful in liquid form and later could be preserved for indefinite periods as such, by using his invention of vacuum jacketed vessels, the range for experimentation was greatly widened. Before recounting these and his engagements with other experts in various fields we must now turn back the pages of his life and mention some of the other events in which he participated.

As one would expect James Dewar joined The Chemical Society early in his career, was a regular attender at its meetings and took part frequently in its discussions. He served as a member of its Council from 1884-1886 and was thrice appointed one of its vice-presidents. His nomination to its presidency caused some discussion, a very rare occurrence in that Society. This was due, in part, to the fact that some members though that although he had scrupulously performed the duties incumbent upon him, he had devoted less time than he might have done to the responsibilities of his Chair in Cambridge University and in part also to his rather brusque manner at times which offended some of his fellow members. A rival candidate, in the person of Sir William Ramsay, was nominated. The result of the election was in James Dewar's favour by 166 votes to 152. Characteristically he showed no resentment at there having been a contest and was as courteous and friendly to his opponents as to his supporters. Indeed, such was the excellent way in which he discharged the duties of his office as President that many who had voted against him said that they regretted having done so. During his presidency a Banquet was given in honour of the past presidents who had completed fifty years membership of The Society (Note 23) at which Professor Friedel of France, one of the many overseas guests, remarked that "there was present the finest phalanx of the Fathers of our Science which exists in this country". Professor Dewar had but one regret. It was that his beloved teacher Lord Playfair had died shortly before the event. During James Dewar's period of office the Journal of the Society was overhauled and a collective index, so necessary for those who wished to pinpoint particular items in past numbers was prepared by Mrs Dougal who had been appointed indexer. It was remarked too by the members that for the first time in many years the Journal appeared in print on the due date and not belatedly, even by several months, as had been happening in previous years. This was brought about by the appointment of a new editor – Mr W. P. Wynne.

In his presidential address the lecturer took the opportunity to range over a wider field than that of his own scientific research and allowed his thoughts to travel into the philosophical and cultural aspects of chemistry, which was unusual for him as he was not so much a theorist as a finder out of facts. In speaking about the relation of scientific research to industry he warned the leaders of industry that although Britain had been for long the workshop of the world her industrial supremacy should not be taken for granted. "It was not an inalienable possession which could be handed down automatically from one generation to another." Its price was eternal vigilance. It was something for which each new generation must strive "and the masters of industry should realise that their greatest ally in the struggle was scientific knowledge". This was a theme which he had very much in his thoughts and to which he recurred frequently in his public utterances as, for example, at a dinner in The Criterion in October 1912, when he stressed the importance of education "which was designed not merely to give men facts but to make them think. Sooner or later the captains of industry must see that training in science was absolutely essential to the management of great industrial undertakings".

An important event in the year 1891 was the celebration of the centenary of the birth of Michael Faraday who, having begun his career as a laboratory assistant in The Royal Institution rose to such eminence as a scientist that he became its chief ornament and pride. For half a century he had served The Royal Institution and among the events commemorating his birth were two public lectures. The first took place on Wednesday 17th June when the Prince of Wales presided. In his remarks as chairman the Prince spoke of Faraday as "a most eminent chemist, a great philosopher and the founder of modern electricity". Professor Tyndall who had known Faraday personally but who was prevented by age and ill health from being present, wrote that, "as Faraday whom he knew, receded from him in time his character became to his mind more and more beautiful". The lecturer was Lord Rayleigh who traced Faraday's career and spoke of his quite outstanding work as a physicist.

The second lecture took place on Friday evening 26th June and was, like the first, attended by a large audience of distinguished scientists. The lecturer was Professor James Dewar. His theme was Faraday's work as a chemist. In the course of his lecture, The Times correspondent informs us that Professor Dewar carried out several experiments with conspicuous success. His lecture, says the writer, "was of an epoch making character in that it realised in fact and with brilliant success the hopes expressed by Faraday in a memorable lecture delivered on 31 January 1845 when he forecast that one day all the gases would be liquefied. During the evening the audience saw liquid oxygen boiling at −180 degrees or nearly 400 degrees below the freezing point of Fahrenheit and was one which Faraday as far back as 1845 hoped to attain. Professor Dewar added that it had been discovered not by experiment but ratiocivinatively that hydrogen boiled at –250 degrees Celsius and that he had verified this by his experimental work. The audience saw alcohol put into the oxygen and in a moment it became solid. When a piece of phosphorus was put into the oxygen nothing followed so that there would seem to be a complete suspension of the chemical affinity. Thus, it would appear that the Lucretian theory could be verified in fact by the proof that at these abnormal temperatures matter suffered actual death. Thus we should have reached the very fundamentals of science. The lecturer was loudly cheered on resuming his seat. The Lord Chancellor proposed the vote of thanks which was seconded by Sir Lyon Playfair who referred 'with pride and gratification that Professor Dewar had been his pupil in chemistry'. Acknowledging the vote of thanks the lecturer humorously related the disastrous consequences which happened in 1884 when he was showing solid oxygen and forgot the presence of liquid ethylene, as he attempted to remove the doubts of a sceptical lady who would NOT believe that it was oxygen. "There was a temporary disappearance of himself and the lady and Dr Warren de la Rue was the only person present who was able to go for a surgeon'. As a result of the accident Professor Dewar had been reduced to inactivity for about six months. Which reminds us that the experiments in which he was engaged were not without hazard. One who was closely associated with him for some years avers that there were occasions when there were explosions and fires. The most serious fire took place when a quantity of ethylene stored in the area at the rear or The Royal Institution caught fire one night and the flames extended to the top of the buildings. The laboratory staff assisted by The

143

London Fire Brigade, put the fire out quickly. But the blaze caused considerable anxiety to the shopkeepers in Old Bond Street which was adjacent to the area. The assurance that extra precautions would be taken assuaged their anxieties. On one occasion a piece of flying metal struck the governor of the gas engine violently and the engine started racing. The mechanic was just in time to turn off the gas and so prevent very serious consequences. Dewar was fond of recounting the incident, always adding that the mechanic who had been through the bombardment of Alexandria said that the explosions at The Royal Institution were worse! On another occasion, after a serious explosion, J. T. Morris tells how next morning he and his brother arrived to find the sensitive Oertling balance had been destroyed and all that could be found among the wreckage were some splinters of mahogany and twisted brass wire. But if there were hazards these were great days, for, adds J. T. Morris, "we were aware that history was being made and that great scientific achievements were being recorded". Experience is a good schoolmaster but sometimes he charges high fees for his instruction.

During the first week of June 1899 celebrations were held to mark the centenary of The Royal Institution which had been gifted to the nation by Count Rumbold. The various events were attended by scientists from all parts of the civilised world who had come to pay science's debt of honour for the benefits which the pure research and the splendid results achieved by those who had worked in its laboratories had conferred upon mankind. The real history of The Royal Institution is the story of the discoveries made by the distinguished scientists who have worked there and notably those of its Directors of Scientific Research. There was Thomas Young who had been one of the prime founders of the wave theory of light. There was Sir Humphrey Davy, an eminent chemist, whose work in "the philosophy of flame" led to the famous invention of the miner's safety lamp which bears his name. There was Michael Faraday who began as a laboratory assistant to Davy and who was often described as Davy's greatest discovery and who during his fifty years of devoted labour in The Institution did a work which was quite unequalled by any scientist both in extent and quality. There was John Tyndall, remembered not only for his contribution to the theory of heat but for the part he played with Darwin and Huxley in the battle which began in the middle of the nineteenth century to make the new standpoint of science acceptable to the layman. And there was now James Dewar who, continuing the work initiated by Faraday on the liquefaction of gases had succeeded by his experiments in proving that, as had been indicated by theory, there is no such thing as a 'permanent' gas for "since his liquefaction of fluorine, helium and hydrogen no known gas remains which has not been reduced to the liquid state"; and who also by his invention of the vacuum jacketed flask had opened entirely new fields for scientific research. As part of the celebrations an interesting exhibition of apparatus used by these and other scientists was staged in the upper library; and a magnificent centenary banquet was held in The Merchant Hall at which the Duke of Newcastle, President of the Royal Institution, presided and at which the principal guest was H.R.H. the Prince of Wales who, in his address of congratulation, recalled that as a boy, along with his father Prince Albert and his brother Prince Alfred, he had attended one of Faraday's lectures forty- five years previously. There was present a large company of eminent scientists from many countries among whom was Sir James Sivewright from South Africa (Note 24) who, a few years later, was to purchase Tulliallan Castle and estate where he spent his retirement years as a loved and highly respected laird. On the evening of 6th June The Lord Mayor of London held a reception for the members of The Royal Institution and their guests. There were also two special lectures where, as on the occasion of the Faraday centenary celebrations the lecturers were Lord Rayleigh and Professor James Dewar. The latter's lecture was unique in that for the first time liquid hydrogen, at once the lightest and the coldest liquid ever known to exist, was seen outside the laboratory of The Royal Institution and was available in such substantial quantities that vessels full of it were handed round for inspection. The lecture was fascinating. Professor Dewar began by stating that his object was to introduce his audience to a new instrument of research – liquid hydrogen. This he exhibited boiling gently in a vacuum tube immersed in liquid air the access of heat being by this precaution greatly impeded. It was a transparent liquid in which there was a whitish deposit, the latter being sold air. To prove that the liquid which he was handling with such freedom was really liquid hydrogen Professor Dewar put a light to a small quantity. A brilliant burst of flame was the result. Of its exceedingly small density he gave an idea by showing that a light material like cork would not float on its surface but sank like lead. Among the other experiments, of which there were several, he showed that oxygen in a sealed tube when lowered into liquid hydrogen quickly became solid and when lifted out it could be seen to become first a liquid and then a gas. Of the

146

temperature of liquid hydrogen Professor Dewar said it was 21 degrees on the Absolute Scale. It had taken him nearly a year to come to a definite conclusion on that point because he could not get any two thermometers to agree. The last part of the lecture was devoted to a dissertation on the extraordinary low vacua obtainable by the use of liquid hydrogen, so perfect that if one end of a closed tube were immersed in it for a short time and then sealed off in the middle, a vacuum was formed in the upper part so perfect that an electrical charge could not be made to pass. Lord Kelvin proposed the vote of thanks, "for a brilliant, beautiful and splendidly interesting lecture". He asked his audience to imagine what would Count Rumford, Davy or Faraday have thought if they could have seen it and heard it. They could not have hoped for their scientific dreams and prophecies to be so splendidly verified within the century". The vote of thanks, we are told, was carried with acclamation. In responding to it Professor Dewar referred in appreciative terms to the part taken in the liquefaction of hydrogen by his assistant Mr Lennox. Speaking on behalf of the overseas visitors Professor Barker said, "how royally they had been entertained listening to lectures such as the world never before had heard and witnessing experiments such as it had never seen". To mark the centenary year Sir James, at his own expense, had the lecture hall beautifully redecorated, a gesture which was much appreciated by the members.

A member of The British Association for the Advancement of Science for more than a quarter of a century and a regular contributor to the discussions at its annual meetings, Professor Dewar was chosen to preside over their conference in 1902. It was an expected and a popular choice. Indeed, many felt that by conferring the highest honour in the academic world of science on one of their most distinguished practitioners The British Association for the Advancement of Science was only doing what had been waiting to be done. The meetings were held in Belfast. The conditions for the conference, centred in the Queen's College and in the Presbyterian College in its immediate vicinity, were ideal and the warm-hearted hospitality of the citizens plus the lavish provision for entertainment and recreation planned by the civic authorities ensured that the visitors would have available all the facilities for the work and leisure which they could desire. The opening meeting was held in the spacious Grosvenor Hall where, according to custom, the President delivered the opening address to a plenary assembly of the members. This was a major event in the career of any scientist as well as a valued honour and like his eminent predecessors Professor Dewar would put much thought and care into its preparation. Introducing the new President his predecessor, Sir Arthur Rucker, said that "Professor Dewar had performed tasks which few were competent to perform. He had carried the heat of scientific battle into the intensest cold, he had attempted to show them what matter was when those restless throbbings we call heat were reduced and as far as possible stilled and the gleams of phosphorescent light he had discovered in these regions were but the symbol of the light he had himself thrown on problems the most difficult and the most profound". Opening his Address with a felicitous reference to the coronation of King Edward VII which had taken place a few weeks previously and which had been postponed from its original date owing to the King's illness which had necessitated a major operation (Note 25), Professor Dewar said that His Majesty owed his recovery both to the skill of his surgeons and to the equipment placed at their disposal by the investigations of science. No one would be more conscious of this than His Majesty himself who had shown a keen interest in The British Association for the Advancement of Science for the past forty- three years and who had only recently been very forthright in a plea for state support for scientific investigation and research, a plea which the present speaker fully endorsed. Thanking the civic authorities for the courtesy and warmth of their welcome to the members attending the conference Professor Dewar made reference to "the broad strides in industrial development, to the great improvement in its harbour and to the handsome civic and educational buildings which had taken place since The British Association had last met in Belfast twenty-eight years ago. Congratulating Andrew Carnegie and other munificent benefactors on the support which they had given to science and education the speaker referred to the outstanding contribution which, over the past century, The Royal Institution, of which he was the present Director, had made to scientific research. From a careful examination of the 'books' he found that the total cost of the maintenance of The Royal Institution was £100,620, and when one recalls the scientific achievements of even four such leaders as Young, Davy, Faraday and Tyndall "you will come to the conclusion that the exceptional man is the cheapest of natural products – the average cost being some £1200 per annum. But the exceptional man is a rare phenomenon. What is needed are more men of the Ph.D. standard who can understand, interpret and use the discoveries made by the men of genius, a field in

149

which the continental nations are outstripping Britain as we shall one day find to our cost industrially and economically." Having made these preliminary points, Professor Dewar turned to the main theme of his address – "the development of that branch of study with which his own labours were most intimately concerned". Mentioning that 'heat and cold' must have engaged the thinking of men from the dawn of history he went on to discuss the nature of cold recounting in a masterly survey the long story of human investigations into "the problem of cold" and related matters. Touching briefly and modestly on his own magnificent contribution to these studies he concluded his Address with the following sentences: "In a legitimate sense all genuine scientific workers feel that they are the inheritors of unfulfilled renown. The battlefields of science are the centres of perpetual warfare in which there is no hope of final victory. But each generation can push the curtain of man's ignorance a little bit further back. To serve in the scientific army, to have shown some initiative and to be rewarded by the consciousness that in the eyes of his comrades he bears the accredited accolade of successful endeavour is enough to satisfy the legitimate ambition of every earnest student of nature. The real warranty that the march of progress in the future will be as glorious as in the past lies in the perpetual reinforcement of the scientific ranks by recruits animated by such a spirit and proud to obtain such a reward." It was a long Address and the reading of it did not end until after 10.30 p.m. but on all sides it was acclaimed as a masterpiece. In seconding the vote of thanks, Professor Sir Frederick Bramwell said that "the only thing that was wanting was any adequate mention of what Professor Dewar himself had done. His innate modesty forbade that." The conference –

or rather the series of group discussion which embrace the entire field of scientific study – lasted for a week and was a period of hectic busyness for the president who, besides paying courtesy visits to each of the groups, participated in the discussions in the chemistry section which was his own particular field of interest. The conference was not all work and no play. Saturday was devoted to recreation when the City Council and local societies hosted special events, the most popular of which was a visit to the Giant's Causeway. On Sunday there were two Services of Divine Worship in the Ulster Hall, morning and afternoon, which accommodated three thousand five hundred and whose seating on both occasions was taxed to the utmost. In the evening there was a lecture for working men in the Grosvenor Hall where there was an audience of fifteen hundred who listened with wrapt attention to Professor Miall whose theme, illustrated with lantern slides, was 'Gnats and Mosquitoes'. In moving a vote of thanks to the lecture Professor Dewar, who presided, said that what they had heard would bring home to all how long and how laborious was the work that lay behind scientific achievement. Monday – which alas! was the only day on which rain fell – was the day chosen for a Garden Party at the Botanic Gardens, and in the evening Professor Dewar presided at a public lecture by Professor Weldon whom he described as "one of the most promising of the young school of zoologists". The title of the lecture was "Inheritance". The concluding meeting on Wednesday night took place in the library of The Queen's Hall. It was an historic occasion in that there was read an invitation from their American counterpart, The American Association for the Advancement of Science, to attend their conference at Washington during the Christmas season. Commending acceptance of it and urging as many of his fellow scientists as possible to attend, Professor Dewar gave it as his opinion that "the great blunder that Englishmen have been perpetuating for many years past was thorough ignorance of what was being done on the other side of the Atlantic. He had over and over again urged on manufacturers that if they would only subsidise their chief officials by a donation which would enable them to spend their holidays in the United States and make themselves acquainted with their great international organisation it would repay them a hundred-fold. He did not think that anything had affected him personally so much as a short visit he paid to America. It was an entirely new revelation to him. He hoped therefore that this Association would be efficiently represented in America on this great occasion at Washington." The Belfast meeting of The British Association for the Advancement of Science had been in every respect most successful. One thousand six hundred and twenty members had attended the meetings. "No town" it was agreed, "can compare with Belfast for hospitality and nowhere is the innate grace and urbanity of the Irish people more widely manifested." Professor Dewar, whose opening address was characterised as being of "permanent value as a history of the efforts which, up till now, have been made to investigate the effects of extremely low temperatures upon gases" was warmly thanked for his services during the conference period and in acknowledging the enthusiastic applause of the audience he said that he attributed the success of the meetings "to the organisation and not to the president" and revealed in a few comments which he made on eminent scientists who had Irish connections that it was his being a pupil of Professor Andrews and Guthrie Tait that led him to undertake the line of research with which his name was connected.

On his way to Belfast, Professor Dewar paid a visit to his nephew Dr Thomas Dewar in Dunblane and on Friday 5th September they, along with other relatives, drove to Kincardine on what was Professor Dewar's first visit to his native town in nearly thirty years. The party put up at the Unicorn Hotel where James Dewar had been born sixty years previously. For him it was a house around which clustered many memories of his parents and his brothers and his own earliest years. Few of his boyhood associates were still alive, but one, William Mustard, a blacksmith, was soon made aware of the professor's arrival by a call at the smithy which used to be a favourite place of resort to all the young Dewars. Scenes and incidents of long ago were recalled and rehearsed with delight. Professor Dewar in the conversation showed that he retained a lively recollection of his early days in Kincardine and notwithstanding his absorbing scientific researches and the fame which his scientific discoveries had brought him it was Willie Mustard's verdict that "he is still the same genial, humble, sincere friend and is still warmly attached to the place of his birth".

In his addresses to The Chemical Society, to The British Association for the Advancement of Science and on other public occasions James Dewar made it plain that the discoveries of those engaged in scientific research should be used by industrialists to enable Britain to enlarge, her share in the international markets. Practising what he was preaching Professor Dewar became an active supporter of The Chemical

Industry Society of which he was a founder member. Inaugurated in June 1881 with two hundred and ninety seven members, it spread rapidly from the metropolis to the provinces, branches being opened in Liverpool, Bristol, Manchester, Birmingham, Newcastle as well as in other manufacturing centres throughout England. A Scottish section was established in 1884 and later on other sections grew up overseas. The original members were connected with widely different aspects of industrial chemistry and included some of the most eminent chemists in Britain. In 1882 a journal was introduced in order to bring the work of researchers and the needs of industrialists into as close proximity as possible. Efforts were also made to encourage the masters of industry to employ in their factories chemists who were educated up to the level of the science of the day and who thus could understand and apply the discoveries of the purely scientific chemists – such as Dewar himself – to particular industries. Industrialists were also urged to erect laboratories which were in every way adequately equipped for the work in which their scientists would be en- gaged. Such an investment in both manpower and equipment was essential if British industry was to keep abreast with and better still pull ahead of its continental rivals, and besides it would prove in the long run economically a prudent investment. To the monthly journal, of which he served on the publications committee for some years, James Dewar was a frequent contributor usually in joint articles with colleagues who were experts in other scientific disciplines. He was a regular attender at the annual conferences of The Society and a delegate to the International Congress of Applied Chemistry held in London in 1909 and which was opened by The Prince of Wales – later King

George V. Having served as one of its vice-presidents James Dewar was elected president for the year 1887-88. During his year of office he submitted to the London section a paper on "The Process for the manufacture of chlorine from chlorine of magnesium" which was described by Professor David Howard as "a most beautiful exemplification of the fact that the highest science may find its application in technical chemistry". On 4th July 1888, at the close of his twelve months' chairmanship Professor Dewar delivered, as was customary, the inaugural address at the annual conference held on this occasion for the first time in Scotland. The venue was Glasgow. Speaking to the assembled members in the university's Bute Hall he began by commenting on the appropriateness of the choice of Glasgow for the conference for "within a very short radius of the city, the industrial metropolis of Scotland, we have the most varied chemical manufacturers probably that can be met within the United Kingdom – not the largest but for variety, for interest and for the ingenuity with which it has been exhibited in connection with their progress during recent years does great credit to Scotland". Stressing, as he was wont to do in his public speeches, the importance of impressing on the community as a whole the fact that our present industrial supremacy is not an inalienable possession which one generation can hand down to another with perfect security, he went on to say that "it is, on the contrary, an unstable possession which can only be maintained and held through scientific intelligence and cultivated industry". Scotland had a great deal to do with the development of chemistry and taking that as his main theme he outlined the contributions of Black, Hutton, James Hall, Dalton, Thomson and Dr Anderson of Glasgow. Referring to

155

the paraffin industry in Scotland and the work of Young he spoke also of the closer attention which was being paid to the utilisation of waste products and nowhere more than in Glasgow. "More and more," he concluded, "we are struck with the idea of this becoming either the petroleum age or the natural gas age, as we can see from the vast petroleum regions in America; and sooner or later we must realise that the supply of energy will be the most telling agents as regards the successful conduct of all our manufactures." Spoken in 1888 these were prophetic words indeed. "Our Society's success is clear from the fact that we have now more than two thousand four hundred members and that it is the largest scientific society in the United Kingdom, omnipresent in most manufacturing areas – a testimony that it is wanted." The speaker was thanked by Professor Dittmar and Sir John N. Cuthbertson and the vote of thanks was carried by acclamation. For the entertainment of the visitors conducted tours of the Art Galleries, of many firms in the area and of The Glasgow International Exhibition were arranged. The Annual Dinner was held in the banqueting hall of the Grand Hotel. Professor Dewar was in the Chair with the Lord Provost seated on his right hand and on his left Professor McKendrick, with whom he had collaborated so happily and fruitfully when James Dewar was a professor in the Veterinary College, Clyde Street, Edinburgh. Lord Provost Sir James King was a director of George McIntosh and Co. which was the oldest chemical firm in Glasgow being founded in 1784 for the manufacture of cudbear (Note 26), which was then a novelty in Glasgow. The toast to the President was proposed by Professor Stanford who described James Dewar as "one of the most distinguished of living chemists, who wherever he might be was a Scotchman first and everything else afterwards". Replying to the toast, Professor Dewar recalled that "many years ago he, as a small boy clad in a kilt had stood admiring Dr Stanford stepping off a steamer – at Kincardine". That he was held in high esteem for his scientific achievements is evident from the fact that The Society presented him with their silver medal in 1918 and when he died the president, Dr E. F. Armstrong, spoke of James Dewar as "perhaps the most brilliant experimentalist of this or any time. … He was an artist in himself, a connoisseur with a love for the good, the beautiful, the uncommon, the interesting and above all for the genuine. As my father – Dr H. E. Armstrong, a colleague and contemporary of James Dewar – wrote me on the news of his death, 'How much our atmosphere has lost of its charm and colour will only be gradually noticed'. Dewar's incursions into industry were many, probably all of the fruitful: 'If we had more Dewars our chemical industry would, today, stand on a different footing'."

The question of water supply to large communities was one which, during the latter decades of the nineteenth century, exercised the minds not only of the civic authorities but of scientists also. The latter were concerned not with quantity and means of distribution but with quality. The discovery of germ life in water and its connection with epidemic disease were matters requiring careful scientific investigation. Experiments on the subject of bacteria and the means of their elimination from water were taking place in America and in Britain. In London much work had been done by Frankland, Crookes and Tidy on all aspects of water supply problems to towns and cities; such as the effect of lead piping, the softening of hard water, the causes for and the elimination of corrosion in boilers, the prevalence of household wells and the need for properly organised communal supplies, harmful micro-organisms in potable water and their removal not only by filtering but by chemical additives and, of course, taste. James Dewar had for many years been interested in these matters and on the death of Dr Tidy he became associated with Sir William Crookes in the daily analysis of the water supplied by The Associated Water Companies of London whose premises were at 14 Colville Road. As London's population grew the need for a reorganisation of the structure of the eight separate Water Boards became apparent. Rationalisation was required. The Water Act of December 1902 made The Metropolitan Water Board responsible for providing the chemical and bacteriological examination of the water supplied to its customers. At the 'appointed day' the water supplied by all the companies was subjected to scrutiny by Sir William Crookes and Professor Dewar. This increased greatly the volume of their work. In 1900 the number of examinations was six thousand seven hundred and thirty one. By 1904 it had risen to nine thousand one hundred and forty six. Requested to report on how to place the examination on a more uniform basis Sire William Crookes and Professor Dewar came to the conclusion, presented to The Metropolitan Water Board in May 1905, that a central laboratory adequately equipped where samples of raw and of filtered water would be thoroughly examined should be erected and that it should be staffed by a full-time officer and assistants. Their recommendation was accepted. New purpose built laboratories were constructed and in July Dr A. C. Houston was appointed as the officer in charge and from 31st October

1905 Sir William Crookes and Professor Dewar were relieved of their responsibilities. By their own report they had made themselves redundant from what had been a very remunerative part-time appointment (Note 27).

To James Dewar the liquefaction of gases was not an end in itself. He always had in view the utilisation of liquid gases in furthering research in different fields of enquiry and so he applied the liquid gases to a wide range of pioneer explorations of the properties of matter at very low temperatures – chemical and photographic action – phosphorescence – and the cohesion and strength of materials. The liquid gases were new tools which science could use and no one was more enthusiastic in using them than Dewar himself. To do so efficiently he had to call in scientists who were authorities in other disciplines and so there began a long and fruitful association with many co-workers in widely different areas of research. Only very lightly can one, in a brief study such as this, touch on this aspect of James Dewar's many activities. One fellow scientist with whom he had a long and profitable partnership was Sir J. Ambrose Fleming with whom he studied electric and magnetic effects such as conduction, thermo- electricity, dielectric constants and magnetic permeability. Like Dewar, Fleming, who is remembered for his invention of the Fleming valve, concerned himself not only with theory, in his case the theory of electricity, but with the practical application of his discoveries. Their collaboration began in the late 1890s and one of the staff recalls how familiar they became with Dewar's loud and hearty greeting to his colleague – "Marnin Fleming" – in his strong Scottish accent. One of Fleming's assistants tells how, with Dewar, Fleming studied the electric resistance of metals and alloys at very low temperatures. The actual resistance coils were made at Fleming's laboratory in University College and brought to The Royal Institution where the resistance of these coils at –78 degrees Celsius and –182 degrees Celsius was measured when liquid air or liquid oxygen were available in quantity. The remarkable drop in resistance was such as to suggest that if the material could be cooled down to the absolute zero of heat, -273 degrees Celsius, all resistance would disappear and the particular metal would achieve perfect conductivity (Note 28). Dewar was very much 'in' on all these and on kindred experiments and together he and Fleming wrote some twenty papers recording their findings in this and in other kindred fields.

With Sir William Crookes, James Dewar made several researches on radium investigating the effects of extreme cold on its emanations (Note 29). Professor Crookes was intensely interested in radioactivity and had it not been for a prolonged stay in South Africa in 1895 he might have anticipated Rontgen in his discovery of X-rays. Dewar's collaboration with Crookes was, naturally, followed up by joint work with Pierre Curie in which they examined the gases occluded or given off by radium and in 1908 Dewar determined the rate at which it evolves helium. In partnership with Professor H. O. Jones of Cambridge James Dewar did some work on iron carbonyls and at a meeting of the Chemistry Section of The British Association for the Advancement of Science in 1907 Professor Jones gave an account of their experiments mentioning that new interesting observations were made and that a new compound of iron and carbon monoxide had been discovered. Professor R. A. Hadfield who, in connection with his father's business, had been concerned with alloys of iron with silicon and manganese and who had prepared a material which came to be used for steel helmets in the Great War collaborated with Professor Dewar on the properties of metals at low temperatures and in problems concerning steel for armour plating and for armour piercing shells. In a lecture to The Royal Society Professor Allan Macfadyan (Note 30) showed that the temperature of liquid air has no appreciable effect upon the vitality of micro-organisms even when they were exposed to a temperature of −190 degrees Celsius for a week. In a subsequent lecture he explained that by the kindness of Sir James Dewar bacteria of many kinds had been subjected to the temperature of liquid hydrogen, -252 degrees Celsius for ten hours. They were sealed in thin glass tubes and introduced directly into liquid hydrogen contained in vacuum jacketed flasks immersed in liquid air. The tubes were then opened and the contents examined microscopically and by culture. The results were completely negative so far as alteration in appearance or in vigour of growth of the micro-organisms went. So, an exposure, he added, of ten hours to a temperature of almost −252 degrees Celsius has no effect on the vitality of micro- organisms. He went on to speak of further similar experiments and Sir James Dewar appears to have conducted them, for, in a lecture on "Inter-planetary bacteria", Professors Shattock and Dudgeon remarked that Sir James Dewar's experiments have demonstrated that while micro-organisms are unharmed by the frozen conditions of liquid air, "the ultra violet rays will kill undried bacteria". At a meeting of the Botany Section of The British Association for the Advancement of Science in 1901 Sir William

Thistleton-Dyer described some experiments of far reaching importance by Professor Dewar on the influence of the temperature of liquid hydrogen on the germinative power of seeds (Note 31). The most important one was that in which five kinds of seeds varying in size and composition were immersed for six hours in liquid hydrogen. "The temperature at which they were cooled was –435 degrees Fahrenheit below melting ice." They were subsequently sown at Kew and germinated readily without exception. In assessing the effect of low temperatures upon metals Professor Dewar showed that lead, tin, iron and also ivory balls when refrigerated gained in elasticity and bounced higher when dropped on an iron anvil than they did before refrigeration. He also demonstrated that the breaking stress of metallic wires was considerably increased as a result of reduction in temperature. Using wires of approximately half an inch in thickness he drew up the following table:

Metal	Temperature	
	15 Celsius	-182 Celsius
	Pounds	*Pounds*
Steel (soft)............................	420	700
Iron...	320	670
Copper....................................	200	300
Brass......................................	310	440
German Silver..........................	470	600
Gold.......................................	255	340
Silver......................................	330	420

The increase in strength is due entirely to the lower temperature for when the wires were restored to their original temperature the increase disappeared. Thus, he argued, the inhabitant of a world where the temperature approximated absolute zero would have much stronger iron and steel with which to build his bridges just as his electric cables would have more perfect conductivity.

Low temperature research brought James Dewar into collaboration once more with his earliest research colleague, with whom he had worked when he was at The Edinburgh Veterinary College, Dr J. G. McKendrick now Professor of Physiology at Glasgow University and also a member of the family circle through his marriage with Mrs Dewar's sister. Dr McKendrick had been engaged in studying the action of cold on microphytes and had found that at the temperature of liquid air though in some cases putrescence was delayed in none was it completely destroyed. Liquid hydrogen provided now the lowest temperature available. In co-operation with James Dewar he froze for an hour, at a temperature of −120 degrees Celsius samples of meat, milk, etc., in sealed tubes. When these were opened after being kept at blood heat for a few days their contents were found to be putrid, thus showing that no matter how low the temperature living organisms are indestructible. Heat can do what cold cannot achieve.

What can be termed an extra mural activity of Professor Dewar was that of being an expert witness in court cases. Such was the calibre of his witness that litigants, especially large companies, were prepared to pay large sums to secure his services which provided him with a very considerable bonus to his somewhat meagre salary. Both he and his friend Sir William Crookes, an equally coveted expert witness, defended their demand for high fees on the ground that, as Sir William expressed it to a firm of law agents, "We who may be looked upon as leaders in the profession owe it to our fellows to charge high and so do our best to counteract the lowering of prices which is so prevalent to the lower branches." (Note 32) Never did he enter a witness box, as Horace says, stans pede in uno. He always did his homework thoroughly. Meticulously prepared and with a thorough mastery of his subject James Dewar was a priceless asset to any litigant and with his alert and brilliant mind he was a formidable witness when it came to cross examination by opposing learned counsel. He was engaged in a very large number of cases, one of the most difficult being the Edison Electric case, in which the Edison Swan Company sought to restrain several others from infringement of their patents in which the evidence was a highly technical and scientific nature and which went on for more than a fortnight. One of the most amusing was the whisky appeal by James Davidge and Thomas Samuel Wells against their conviction for unlawfully selling Scotch and Irish whisky "not of the nature, substance and quality demanded". James Dewar's evidence based both on scientific analysis and on his personal experience of having "tasted all varieties of whisky from the days of my youth" and his ripostes to the Q.C.s who were questioning him makes highly entertaining reading, and reveals a witness who is at least a match for his questioners. From these two cases alone one can well see why a litigant was eager to have James Dewar espouse his case.

As science is international it is of vital importance that the terms used by scientists in every country should have exactly the same meaning. How else can scientists speak to each other across the dividing walls of nationality and language? How else can they co-operate in research and ensure that their discoveries are made available in the commercial world and on the factory floor. A standard nomenclature when terms are fixed in meaning, where they are permanent, universal and acceptable to all is essential. In the latter half of the nineteenth century when electricity and telegraphy were leaping across all national barriers, when electrical measurements were of daily occurrence not only in scientific laboratories but in factories and workshops in which the manufacturer of electrical and telegraphic apparatus was carried out, it became a matter of grave and urgent importance that a standard vocabulary of measurement should be established. Thus ohms, volts, amperes, coulombs – to name but a few terms – had to mean the same everywhere. It was also important that there should be agreed a standard of light with reference to which various electrical and other lights could be measured. With this in view the first International Electrical Exhibition was held in Paris in the autumn of 1881 (Note 33). It was sponsored by the French government who invited to it the leading scientific and electrical specialists of all countries whose business it was to meet in conference with a view to discussing many important questions connected with electricity and telegraphy and in particular to establish an international system of units for expressing the results of electrical measurements and of their research. Among the British representatives at this the first of several such conferences was Professor James Dewar. In 1908 there was another 'first' in Paris, this time the first International Congress of the Cold Storage Industries held in the Grand Palais. One of the sections concerned itself with questions relating to low temperatures and their general effects, at which the principal speaker was Sir James Dewar. Although he had received many honours from learned societies, including an honorary Ll.D. from all four Scottish Universities – the only person to have done so – and though he was in future years to be the recipient of still further honours there came to him in 1904 the honour of a knighthood. While this signal mark of Royal favour and of national recognition of his unique services to science and through his research to the nation as a whole gave much pleasure to his colleagues, many of them, in later years, expressed their disappointment that it had not been followed by the award of The Order of Merit, the highest honour in the gift of sovereign and one which in their opinion he richly merited. In 1913 Sir James, as he must now be designated, published a notable paper showing that the mean atomic specific heats of the elements between the boiling points of liquid nitrogen and hydrogen exhibited, when plotted in terms of their atomic weights, a definite periodic variation instead of being approximately uniform as they are at ordinary temperatures. This was almost his last piece of freelance research before everything was called to a halt by the outbreak of The Great War in August 1914, after which all the nation's resources, material and human, were mobilised for war work. The Royal Institution had from its inception been dedicated to disinterested scientific research with sufficient funds, obtained principally through donations, (Note 34) to finance its work. Now funds dried up. Members of the staff were conscripted for national service. All the resources of The Royal Institution were directed towards serving the immediate national emergency and no longer was Sir James able to follow his own sweet will in matters of research. For him, the war years became a trying time. Not only – like Othello – was his occupation gone but he shared the anxieties common to all thoughtful men during those fateful and dangerous years and suffered, as was to be expected of a man of his sensitive nature, bouts of depression at the contemplation of the awful carnage and especially the slaughter of young life which the war entailed. Though now seventy-two years of age he was mentally as fit as ever he was. So it was surprising that the government did not make more use of his unique abilities particularly in view of the fact that as long ago as 1888 he had been associated with Sir Frederick Abel (Note 35) in the invention of cordite, a smokeless fuel, which had been of immense benefit to both the army and the navy. Appointed by Earl Stanhope, the Secretary for War, along with Sir Frederick Abel and Professor Dupré, the latter of whom took little or no part in the affair, to examine the use of high explosives, Abel and Dewar quickly came to the conclusion that a better material than gun cotton was necessary and that none of the substitutes submitted by manufacturers were suitable. Accordingly, they devised, and in 1890 patented in favour of the Secretary of War, a new explosive compounded of gun cotton and nitroglycerine in cords or thread – hence the name cordite – which after exhaustive tests by the Director of Artillery, was found to be superior to anything so far possessed by the military authorities. All the tests resulted in its favour. Sent out to the northern regions of Canada and to India where it was tested under conditions of extreme cold and heat, and subjected to conditions of humidity in damp climates it was pronounced to possess better qualities than any other explosive. In announcing its acceptance by the government Mr Campbell Bannerman, who had succeeded Earl Stanhope, paid tribute to the two inventors in these words: "You may search not only this country but the world and not find two men more qualified to decide any question such as was submitted to them." It is indeed surprising then that Sir James was not enlisted into full-time war service but bureaucracy probably thought, not knowing their man, that at the age of seventy-two he was too old to be useful for regular employment. In 1915 he was, however, called in by Lord Haldane, to advise on a particular problem about cordite and also to bring his exceptional knowledge to bear on the development of metal-jacketed containers for liquid oxygen to enable pilots to fly at very high altitudes. It also must have been a consolation to him to have known that his work with charcoal as an absorbent for gases was of great value in the designing of the gas masks which enabled our soldiers to withstand the gas attacks of the Germans which were launched during the second battle of Ypres.

In order to employ his days profitably he turned to one of his first loves and one on which he had delivered his first series of Christmas lectures to juveniles – Soap Bubbles and Soap Films. On March 17th, 1916, The Times carried an article entitled. "A Long Lived Soap Bubble", in reference to a soap bubble which Sir James had exhibited on the previous afternoon during a lecture and which he had blown on 17th February. It was as perfect as it had been on the day on which it was made. It was a glowing sphere of iridescent colours without the slightest trace of blackness, which is the prelude to disintegration. Its longevity was due to the fact that it was blown in and filled with clean air which was completely free from the motes and small particles which, with soap bubbles, are the seed of decay. Unfortunately it came to an untimely end about ten days later due to the vibration occasioned when the equipment for producing liquid air for Sir J. J. Thomson's Saturday afternoon lecture was being set up. Other bubbles of Sir James's creation withstood the vibration, one of them being completely black and showing no colour at all. Four days later being blown with hydrogen it lost all colour. It was five-and-a-quarter inches in diameter and the thickness – or thinness – of its skin was about a ten-millionth of an inch. Yet it was strong enough to support a drop of soap solution hanging from its lowest point. Another bubble blown with air and three- and-a-half inches in diameter took longer than the one blown with hydrogen to become black. In his experiments with soap bubbles, and they were many, Sir James was not just engaging in self-amusement or trying, for the fun of it, to see what would happen under various conditions. There was a serious side to his experimentation. From his observations he noticed that in a sealed exhausted tube the upper portion became black leaving a lower coloured section with a sharply defined horizontal edge. When he tilted the tube the coloured section responded at once. The film then could be used as a level and it was his hope that an instrument could be devised along these lines to enable air pilots to keep their 'planes on an even keel. Though it did not work out as he had hoped the possibilities were there where such a level, responding instantaneously and free from unsteadiness could be invented and become a valuable instrument at the disposal of air pilots.

169

After Sir James had concluded his Friday evening lecture on 21st June 1921 the Duke of Newcastle, who was in the Chair, spoke of the pleasing duty he had now to perform in view of the approaching Golden Wedding of Sir James and Lady Dewar. "Sir James's name," said the Duke, "was not only a household name with all of us but it is no great exaggeration to say that every one of us utilises in some way or other the results of the great discoveries which he has made during the last forty or fifty years." Speaking of Sir James's early investigations in the physiology of the eye and the long series of spectroscopic researches which he had carried out with Professor Living at Cambridge, which had made both their names famous, and of his collaboration with Sir Frederick Abel in the invention of cordite which the army and navy have used ever since, he said it was to that that "our victory in the war was largely due". Referring to Sir James's immense contribution to the liquefaction of the gases the Duke reminded his audience that liquid air was "now a commercial article, and to prove its value we have only to look at the attempt which is now being made to ascend Mount Everest, an attempt which would have been absolutely impossible if it were not for that invention. If that attempt succeeds it will be due not only to the skill, experience and intrepidity of the explorers but to the inventive genius of Sir James Dewar. In the last forty-four years Sir James has delivered more than fifty Friday evening lectures, more than thirty-six sets of lectures covering the whole range of chemistry and chemico-physics – nine sets of Christmas lectures to juveniles, firmly establishing in the minds of the rising generation a foundation of scientific study." Expressing his thanks to Lady Dewar for the support she had given to Sir James, without which his

170

achievements would not have been possible, the Duke mentioned particularly the hospitality which she dispensed to those who attended the Friday evening discourses. On behalf of the members of The Royal Institution the Duke then presented Sir James and Lady Dewar with a beautiful Golden Loving Cup. On rising to reply Sir James was received with rousing cheers. Having thanked the members of The Royal Institution for their beautiful and generous gift and having acknowledged gratefully his indebtedness to his wife for "All she had been and done through their harmonious life of togetherness for fifty years", he mentioned his love of music "and the early vanity which impelled me to make my own music, which was a little insane". He had available the fiddle he made and signed in 1854, "my first authentic signature", and which would be played that evening by two young ladies. Reminiscing on his years at The Royal Institution he felt that he had been overburdened with honours. "My work has been an absolute pleasure and delight to me. It has never engendered in me a though of anticipating any reward. The crown of science is the joy of its cultivation, as Shakespeare has it, from whom, through the mouth of Cerimon in Pericles, the qualities of the physician, in these days the only scientist, are delineated:

I held it ever,
Virtue and cunning were endowments greater (Note 36)
Than nobleness and riches: careless heirs
May the two latter darken and expend;
But immortality attends the former
Making a man a god. 'Tis known I ever
Having studied physick, through which secret art

By turning o'er authorities, I have
(Together with my practice) made familiar
To me and to my aid, the blest infusions
That dwell in vegetives, in metals, stones:
And I can speak of the disturbances
That nature works, and of her cures, which give me
A more content in course of true delight
Than to be thirsty after tottering honour,
Or tie my treasure up in silken bags
To please the fool – and death."

Act III. Sc. II

He had served under three Dukes of Newcastle, as Presidents of The Royal Institution to whose unflagging support both The Royal Institution and he himself owed so much. His own devotion to The Royal Institution was matched by that of his wife. During the war she was plagued with poor health and "I was anxious" he said "to get her to move to Cambridge because, as I told her, the Germans would never bomb Cambridge. But nothing would induce her to leave The Institution." At the conclusion of his speech Sir James invited the audience to partake of Lady Dewar's and his hospitality "and to hear my fiddle played".

As early as 1872 James Dewar had become interested in the calculation of solar temperature, an interest which was resurrected in the closing years of his life. He now began to apply an ingeniously designed charcoal thermoscope – a modification of the one he had made more than forty years previously – to discover the radiation from the sky by both day and night: from the sun at all seasons of the year and during an eclipse, as well as from the moon, the clouds and the stars. This thermoscope was erected immediately below a sliding panel in the roof of one of the laboratories of The Royal Institution. There, in his small private observatory, even when beyond his eightieth birthday, Sir James kept solitary vigil watching the heavens at all hours, and recording the varying radiation through the changing sequences of weather conditions. It was thus that his friend of many years, Professor Armstrong, saw him for the last time late on a March evening of 1923. That night Sir James fell suddenly ill and on March 20th he passed away. This last meeting was the picture, says Professor Armstrong, which "was the one above all others he liked to cherish of his old dear friend, as a silent watcher of the skies and a life-long seeker after truth". The scene reminds us of what was said of another celebrated explorer, Mallory, who kept pushing his way upwards on the slopes of the as yet unconquered Mount Everest, "Last seen, making for the top".

The tidings of Sir James Dewar's death, though at the advanced age of eighty-one, evoked many expressions of sorrow and a multitude of tributes to his genius and character. The first message of sympathy received by Lady Dewar came, through Lord Stamfordham, from King George V and Queen Mary. It read: "The King and Queen have heard with much regret of the death of Sir James Dewar and desire me to express their true sympathy with you in your loss – a loss which will be shared by the whole world of science." All the national newspapers contained extensive obituaries in which were outlined his distinguished career and his unique contributions to numerous aspects of scientific research and in particular to chemistry. The Times, after referring to him as "one of the most brilliant experimentalists of his time" proceeded to have a detailed account of his principal scientific achievements and concluded with a list of the many honours conferred upon him by universities at home and abroad and by scientific societies in his native land and overseas. In a Third Leader - and to be made the subject of this is rare distinction – the editor wrote that for The Royal Institution "to have found one man with a combination of gifts so well fitted for its objects was great good fortune". Commenting on how, for more than forty years, the Londoners who were interested in science had enjoyed "the resonant voice, the logical statement and the technical wizardry of the plump and bearded high priest of Albermarle Street", the writer added that "all who within that period themselves had to address the exacting audiences of The Royal Institution must cherish a warm memory of the crisp and kindly encouragement Dewar used to give them in the trying few minutes before their lecture began. In pure science Dewar was best known by the methods he devised for approaching the absolute zero of temperature and for his study of the behaviour of elements and compounds under conditions so far removed from their normal state in the familiar world... In private life he was a genial host and an interesting companion. He was a fine musician and his collection of objets d'art was noted with admiration even by professional experts. His skill as an expert witness became almost a legend of the courts. He was a great man, vigorous, kindly and combative." The two national news- papers in his native Scotland – The Scotsman and The Glasgow Herald – also had long and laudatory obituaries. The one in The Glasgow Herald was written by his old friend Professor

Andrew Gray. In the course of a detailed account of the splendour of Sir James's achievements Nature, the science magazine, had this to say: "Our scientific edifice is by his death deprived of one of its main pillars. We shall not easily appraise the loss. The immensity and sustained originality of his genius, the service he rendered to our civilisation can be but insufficiently appreciated outside the small circle of intimates who witnessed his work and who penetrated through the thick mask of modesty and reticence which he habitually wore... At heart he was full of human sympathy, a most gentle and loveable nature." Cambridge University ended its generous tribute with this sentence: "As an experimentalist Dewar stood alone: there has never been a greater; probably none so great."

In his will, he stated that "being a member of The Cremation Society he desired his body to be cremated, the funeral arrangements to be of a simple character and kept entirely private and confined to members of his family". The cremation, we are told in The Times of 2nd April, took place at Golders Green. "There was no service, no congregation, no ceremony of any kind. Before the cremation a service was held in his home at The Royal Institution at which the Bishop of Worcester officiated. And meanwhile the staff paid their last tribute to him at a simple service in his study at The Royal Institution conducted by his old friend Canon Carnegie. The members of the family alone attended at Golders Green." The Maharaj Rama of Ihalawar, a friend and great admirer of Sir James "paid him a last tribute of regard by a call of condolence at The Royal Institution on Saturday morning. His Highness is recovering from a severe illness and is hardly able to walk". The net value of his estate was £128,828. He bequeathed to Cambridge University all his scientific equipment in the laboratory there and made a similar bequest to The Royal Institution. He left a sum of £500 to be distributed in cash or gifts to his assistants who had been with him since 1900 and a similar sum to three of his colleagues who were asked to publish, as advisers to Lady Dewar, such of his scientific papers as might be considered worthy of publication. He desired that "no Bursary, Fellowship, Scholarship, Annual Lecture or any other memorial be founded or connected with his name by public subscription and that no biography of his life should be published as a separate book". Though aware of his wish that no public memorial should be erected to his memory the members of The Royal Institution felt that they would in no way contravene that desire by placing a memorial plaque on the staircase wall of The Institution. So on 12th November 1925 a plaque designed by Sir Bertram MacKinnal was unveiled. It is in itself an attractive work of art worthy of a man whose love for the arts came only second to his devotion to science. In accepting the plaque the Duke of Newcastle referred to Sir James Dewar as one of the greatest men of science of this epoch, a man whose life and example were a priceless legacy to The Royal Institution and would be an inspiration to all who came within its walls. Sir J. J. Thomson, Master of Trinity College, Cambridge, spoke of how Sir James had ever delighted them with the amazing beauty of his experiments. "He was an artist to his fingertips. He was essentially an investigator and a pioneer. Three of his discoveries could not be passed over in any tribute.

(1)   To Dewar they owed the use of liquefied gases as a physical agent, (2) the vacuum flask was not only an important scientific instrument but had largely added to the amenities of life who were unaware to whom they owed it. (3) Of special importance was his discovery of the method of producing high vacua by means of charcoal cooled by liquid gas to which the advance of modern physics was in no small measure due." If Sir James's devotion to The Royal Institution was total it was emulated by that of Lady Dewar whose home it had been for most of their married life. On vacating their flat, after her husband's death, she left as a parting gift the beautiful and expensive fittings which she and Sir James had installed.

"He who writes of men of science," says Thomas Martin in his biography of Michael Faraday, "must recognise that their lives are uneventful in the general estimation. Their discoveries seldom excite any immediate popular interest. Great scientific achievements pass unremarked at the time and the truths the scientist states are usually above the comprehension of the man in the street. Scientific research is the least dramatic of human occupations; patience and perseverance are the qualities it calls for. Its moments of triumph come in the seclusion of the laboratory." But it is not the passing moment, it is the page of history that is the test of greatness and the greatness of Michael Faraday as of his admirer and successor at The Royal Institution, James Dewar, the verdict of history leaves us in no doubt.

Notes

1.   A daughter of Hugh Eadie, Shipowner, Kincardine, she died on 18th March 1852 - Clackmannan Advertiser, 27/03/1852.

2.   The first recorded meeting of the managers of the U.P. congregation took place on 1st March 1852. Arrangements were made to provide a library for the minister and on 5th April Thomas Dewar and William Norrie were appointed to catalogue the books which were to be the property of the congregation. When on 4th February 1855 the "Body of managers was reconstituted to consist of thirteen member" among those elected were Thomas Dewar and Robert Maule. – Minutes, 1852f.

3.   The report of a complimentary dinner to Mr Adam, M.P., on November 15th , 1851, is typical of the references made to the catering in the Unicorn Hotel. "The large room was tastefully decorated. The viands, wines and fruits for the occasion did great credit to Mr Dewar by whom the dinner was served." This comment is typical of those which followed an account of similar occasions held at The Unicorn Inn.

4.   Mr Thomas Dewar had a private gas works for the lighting of the Inn long before the Gas Works – i.e. the plant of the Kincardine Gas Company – were in operation. – Alloa Advertiser, September 10th 1898.

5.   The Subscription School was non-denominational and was attended by the children of parents, many of whom were

not members of the Established Church and who wished to opt out of the Parish Church School. Subscription Schools were fairly common in nineteenth century Scotland. There were 450 in 1857. Some were provided by enlightened employers for the children of their employees, though not exclusively so; and others, as in Clackmannan, by the workers where at each of the three pits there was a Subscription School. The academic success of the school depended entirely on the teacher, and among teachers at that time there was a great range of knowledge and ability from those who were little more than literate to those who were quite scholarly. Mr Hogg was the teacher in 1852. By 1855 Alexander Dewar had become the teacher. In August of that year when the pupils were examined by the Presbytery "in the presence of the directors and many parents, the pupils acquitted themselves so well that it was clear that in Mr Dewar the directors had secured an intelligent, energetic and efficient teacher. Mr Dewar has only been one session in charge of the school but the way in which he performed his duties augurs well for the future prosperity of the institution." – Clackmannan Advertiser, August 18th, 1855. On November 6th, 1858, the Alloa Advertiser intimated that "Mr Dow of Culross has entered upon his duties of teacher in The Subscription School in consequence of Mr Dewar, the former teacher, intending to follow the medical profession." Was Mr Dow ill equipped to teach mathematics and less knowledgeable than young James Dewar – which led naturally to the young lad's acquiring a distaste for the local school? One recalls how young Thomas Carlyle's teacher, Sandy Beattie, in Ecclefechan, was unable to teach his pupil Latin and Thomas had to repair to his minister for instruction in that subject; and how Dr Adams of

179

Cambridge said of Samuel Johnson – now a university student – "I was his nominal tutor; but he was above my mark". All three: Dewar, Carlyle and Johnson were men of genius.

6.   On 26th September 1857, The Alloa Advertiser carried a long advertisement giving details of the accommodation furnishings, etc. In addition to the usual business of an inn and hotel to which was added catering for special functions, The Unicorn was also the place where coaches running between Dunfermline and Falkirk changed horses. The new proprietor, Mr Clark, tried to develop the tourist trade, pointing out in his advertisement (q.v. in subsequent copies of the newspaper) the many places of interest which were easily accessible to visitors. Also 1858: May 15th – Sale of Furniture and horses, etc., at Unicorn Inn; July 31st – Sale of growing crop; August 14th – Houses in Kilbagie Street, Police Station; November 27th – Large stock of salt belonging to the late Mr T. Dewar.

7.   Dr Kirk taught Hindustani because of the number of pupils who aspired to service – government or mercantile – in the Far East. – The Dollar Magazine.

8.   Cf. 'The Report' in The Alloa Advertiser.

9.   For this section cf. The Edinburgh Veterinary College Council Minutes 1866-1870. J. G. McKenrick. "The Story of My Life" and William Dick (1793-1866) in The Veterinary Review, Vol. IV.

10.   The Records of The Royal Society of Edinburgh and J. G. McKendrick, "The Story of My Life".

11.   After graduating M.D. Alexander Dewar became a doctor in Melrose. On the departure of Dr I. G. Smith, the Medical Officer, to London, he was elected at a meeting of The Parochial Board on 10th February 1869, as Medical Officer at Melrose. On May 26th 1875 he resigned in order to become Physician at the Waverley Hydropathic Establishment which in these days was a very popular institution. It was extended in 1876 to meet "the greatly increasing number of visitors". Socially he continued to cultivate his boyhood interest in curling and was, in 1873, President of the Melrose Curling Club (Border Advertiser). Like his brothers, Ebenezer and Hugh, who emigrated to Australia, to Sydney and Melbourne respectively. Alexander eventually made his home in that continent. He died at Crown Terrace, Sydney on 14th February 1906. Ebenezer, more than any of the others, retained his connection with his native town and during the last thirteen years of his life he remitted annually a sum of money to his friends in Kincardine to provide coals for the most necessitous members of the community. After his death, on 19th July 1898, that benefaction was continued by his widow. Robert Menzies carried on a successful drapery business in Kincardine and it was with him that James made his home after the sale of the Unicorn Hotel. On 17th January 1860 Robert married Eliza Scott the youngest daughter of Mr William Thomson, Charlotte Villa, Sciennes Hill, Edinburgh. Thomas, the oldest brother, went into the wine and spirit trade in Edinburgh.

12.   Highland and Agricultural Society – Directors' Meeting 1873f.

13.   In earlier years there had been widespread dishonesty practiced by many suppliers of chemical manures. In an advertisement in 1860 the Kilbagie Chemical Manure Company referred to "the heartless swindle of manure companies selling trash and worse under the name of chemical manures". The scientists of the Highland and Agricultural Society played a notable part in stamping out such dishonesty and in ensuring that farmers were supplied with a product which would give their soil what it required".

14.   He concluded his letter with this sentence, "I still trust, however, that the Society will ultimately see that this office of Chemist will never be properly filled except by one thoroughly trained in scientific research and this, the making him a real agricultural chemist will depend on the means placed at his disposal for applying his scientific knowledge to agriculture." – Nature, Vol. XII.

15.   Interestingly enough Dr J. G. McKendrick the friend and collaborator of his early years was to marry James Dewar's sister-in-law in 1867.

16.   John Fuller, a wealthy and somewhat eccentric M.P. endowed the Fullerian Chair of Chemistry at The Royal Institution in February 1833. The first occupant of the Chair was Michael Faraday at salary of £100 per annum.

17.   The Royal Institution was founded in 1799 by Benjamin Thomson, Count Rumford, not only to provide facilities for scientific research but even more to encourage scientists, by giving popular lectures, to communicate to the

reasonably intelligent non-specialist members of society what they, as scientists, were doing.

18.   In his book, Fifty Years at The Royal Institution, Mr Ralph Cory records two incidents which are worth mentioning. Sir James, he says, had a very attractive and active personality even on to what we call old age. "Coming into the Library one day he found Dr Forbes reading. 'Hullo! how are you?' Dewar exclaimed, 'Oh, as well as can be expected at my age,' Forbes replied. 'At your age,' said Dewar, 'how old are you?' 'Well, I'll soon be seventy' said Forbes. 'Seventy!' exclaimed Dewar giving him a slap on the back that nearly made him collapse. 'You're only a boy! Look at me – I'm eighty!' – and out he went humming a tune. 'Sir James Dewar was a close friend of Sir James Crichtone-Browne. One day, after being upstairs with Dewar, Crichtone-Browne said to me 'You know, Corry, Sir James is getting old and I have to watch him closely'. A little later, Sir James Dewar came out of his office and said of Crichtone-Browne almost exactly what he had said of Dewar."

19.   Fleming's book on Ripples and Waves is an interesting example of one lecturer's course of addresses to a juvenile audience.

20.   Nature, Vol. XVII.

21.   One recalls the delighted amazement of the explorers on first seeing the Pacific Ocean enshrined in Keats' sonnet "On First Looking into Chapman's Homer":

"Then felt I like some watcher of the skies
When some new planet swims into his ken:
Or like stout Cortez – when, with eagle eyes
He stared at the Pacific, and all his men
Look'd at each other with a wild surmise,
Silent, upon a peak in Darien."

22.   'And let it be also remarked that without the means of making high vacua the incandescent lamp, which for long was such a boon to familes on winter nights, would have been impossible." – Fifty Years of Electricity, Ambrose Fleming.

23.   It is interesting to observe that when, in 1921, the past presidents of The Society were invited to the celebration of another anniversary dinner as guests of honour the oldest was Sir James Dewar who had been elected to membership almost fifty-one years previously.

24.   Sir James Sivewright purchased the Estate of Tulliallan from the Marquis of Lansdowne in the spring of 1901.

25.   King Edward had undergone what was then regarded as a serious operation – for appendicitis.

26.   Cudbear – an agent used in dyeing. This purple or violet powder came from various species of lichen and it was valuable in dyeing ruby and maroon shades as well as a variety of browns. In his speech the Lord Provost mentioned that he was a director of George McIntosh and Company which was associated with The Hurlet and Campsie Alum Company. It had been established in 1784 by a Highlander

who brought his workforce from the north and as none of them could speak English there was no danger of their betraying trade secrets. He ruled his small squad of workers with military discipline and every man had to be indoors by 8 p.m. or else was fined 1/- for being late. The members of the conference also visited the Nobel Explosives Factory with which Sir James had a twenty-year connection – Glasgow Herald, July 5/6/7, 1888.

27.   Biography of Sir William Crookes – E. E. Fournier d'Albe, and The Minutes of the Metropolitan Water Board.

28.   This remains a subject for scientific research. As late as October 1987 Dr Alex Mueller, Switzerland, was awarded a Nobel Prize for discovering a new ceramic material which can conduct electricity with no resistance. The new material is based upon oxygen and copper capable of conducting an electric current without resistance at –238 degrees Centigrade, i.e. 12 degrees Centigrade higher than anything previously known.

29.   Nature, Vol. LCCIX.

30.   Dr Alan McFadyan, who was Director of the Jenner Institute of Preventive Medicine, wrote, "The fact that life can continue to exist under such conditions (-252 degrees Centigrade) affords new ground for reflection as to whether after all life is dependent for its continuance on chemical reactions. We as biologists follow with the keenest interest Professor Dewar's heroic attempts to reach the absolute zero of temperature… He has already placed in our hands an agent of investigation from the effectiveness of which we who are

working on the subject at least hope to gain a little further insight into the great mystery of life itself." – February 1901.

31.   Among the seeds used were: pea, vegetable marrow, mustard, barley.

32.   Letter to W. C. Robertson Austen.

33.   Speaking at a later conference in 1908, The President of the Board of Trade, Mr Winston Churchill, reiterated that internationally agreed standards were of vital importance and said, "they must be definitely fixed in value, they must be permanent and be a universal system acceptable to all".

34.   A regular and generous donor to the cold temperature research in which Sir James was particularly interested was his nephew, Dr Thomas Dewar, Dunblane.

35.   Sir Frederick Abel, ordinance chemist at Woolwich and the Government's chief authority on all matters dealing with explosives.

36.   Cunning means knowledge in this context.

Additional Notes

One of the best known local violin makers in the nineteenth century was William Mackay who was born in 1815 and who was still active in 1899. In all he made about 50 violins, 6 violincellos and 6 violas. His violins were covered with yellow varnish, bore no label or date but had written inside the back, "William Mackay, Crosshill, Kincardine on Forth".

Absolute Zero

The lowest temperature on the Kelvin thermometer scale is – 273.16 degrees Celsius or –459.69 degrees Fahrenheit. The Kelvin Scale is the standard for all scientific temperature measurements. This temperature is the one which matter would have if ALL heat were removed from it and is therefore the lowest possible temperature. A temperature of absolute zero can never be reached but only approached. In his scientific experiments Sir James Dewar was gradually approaching it – but still had some way to go. "A few millionths of a degree above absolute zero is the lowest ever attained so far in a laboratory" (Encyclopaedia Americana).

Tribute By The Royal Institution

At a meeting of the members of The Royal Institution on Mon- day, 9th April, 1923, a tribute was paid to Sir James Dewar which, inter alia spoke of how nobly he had "maintained and enhanced the fame of The Royal Institution and by his invaluable discoveries had made contributions of incalculable and far-reaching value to the wealth and welfare of mankind. … His whole- hearted devotion to science like his predecessor Faraday, his remarkable skills in experimental research and lecture demonstrations." His researches which had lasted over a period of more than fifty years were summed up under seven headings, the honours conferred upon him were listed, his skill in arranging courses of lectures not only on every branch of science but also on different branches of literature and the arts was recorded and the tribute concluded by making reference to his devotion to the welfare of The Royal Institution itself, his generous donations to the Fund for Experimental Research, his frequent presentation of books to the library and his paying for the complete redecoration and refurbishment of the Lecture Room to mark his completion of a period as long as Faraday's as Fullerian Professor of Chemistry – thirty-four years.

The resolution approving the tribute was moved by the Duke of Newcastle. His Grace said: "By his death we have lost one of the great world figures of science and a very faithful and devoted member of this Institution and all of us feel too that we are mourning the loss of a great personal friend. His name stands second to none in the list of great names who have conferred honour on The Royal Institution and with our sorrow is mingled pride in his achievements." The resolution was seconded by Sir James Crichton-Browne who said: "It may be affirmed that no greater British man of science has lived during the last fifty years. ... His career at The Royal Institution has been a succession of triumphs. Here it was he carried out his researches on the liquefaction of gases and on the properties of matter at close to the absolute zero liquefying and then solidifying in turn air, oxygen, fluorine and hydrogen elucidating at the same time the effects of the low temperatures reached on magnetic powers, on electrical conductivity, on the tensile strength of metals, on chemical and photographic action and on living organisms. Here it was that he produced cordite, that he invented the vacuum jacket, that he utilised the absorptive powers of carbon and revealed the iridescent marvels of the soap bubble. These researches were conducted not without risk to life and limb... His services here have been practically gratuitous. His emoluments have never exceeded £300 per annum. On two hundred and three occasions in all – in forty-eight Friday evening discourses... one hundred and seventeen afternoon lectures... thirty-eight Christmas lectures – to rapt and overflowing audiences – he described his excursions into the hidden arcane of Nature and has shown us, in exquisite experiments, the treasures he brought back... Medium of height and slight of build he had a charming and approachable manner which won him a host of friends. He had a very attractive personality. Bright, breezy, open-hearted and not without the saving grace of humour he was one of the most lovable of men, always accessible to the student, full of encouragement for the honest worker, brimful of knowledge and as generous with his brains as with his purse." ... On a personal note Dr Chrichton-Browne spoke of his having known Sir James for fifty years: "their friendship had never known a jar and had ripened into almost fraternal relations". Sir Ernest Rutherford spoke of Sir James Dewar "as a heroic figure in science, one of the greatest experimenters of our age". He had a great admiration for Sir James as a scientist, a deep affection for his personal qualities and treasured the remembrance of his many acts of kindness.

The Resolution, moved by the Duke of Newcastle, was then put to the meeting and adopted unanimously, all the members standing while it was read.

Grand Discovery

Air is so condensed and congealed that it becomes visible as a sky-blue liquid – that is the latest marvel of science. The discoverer of the process is Professor James Dewar who explained it at The Royal Institution. He liquefies nitrous oxide or ethylene by subjecting them to a temperature respectively of 162 and 180 degrees of frost; then by allowing these volatile elements to evaporate in the presence of their own liquids he produces a still greater degree of coldness. By ethylene, for instance, a temperature can be obtained equal to 31.8 degrees below the freezing point and at this with a pressure of 750 lbs to the square inch the oxygen and nitrogen of the air pass into a liquid state. The audience actually beheld liquid oxygen in a little globe. The professor hopes to get yet farther and to produce solid air. He has only to increase the degree of coldness and atmospheric pressure. He was used this liquid air already so as to produce a vacuum with only a small fraction of a millioneth of an atmosphere of gas pressure and this becomes a new agent of investigation by means of which it is hoped the nature of the electric current may yet be detected. If the sun were to be extinguished, we know from this beautiful discovery that the air would tumble to the ground and form a liquid layer thirty-five feet deep, of a beautiful blue colour: and if all the universal suns were also quenched the liquid would probably become solid. Even as it is, ice is, compared with the liquid air, twice as hot as boiling water is to ice.

Alloa Advertiser, February 25th, 1893.

Liquid Air for Export

Professor Dewar has successfully conveyed a considerable quantity of liquid air from London to Cambridge, where it was appropriate exhibited at Peterhouse, the College which always must be associated with the great scientific work of Cavendish. The liquid air reached Cambridge with only a trifling loss of bulk, notwithstanding the incessant jolting of the train.

Alloa Advertiser, November 25th, 1893.

Robert Maule, J.P and his son Sir Robert

Robert Maule

Sir Robert Maule

They were good men and the Christ was in them.

"Meet me at Maule's"

Biographies

In eighteenth century Scotland, there was no more familiar or kenspeckle figure than the itinerant tailor who, with the tools of his trade, travelled from farm to farm working in the homes of his customers for a monetary payment of 8d. a day along with free meals and a bed. In exchange for that remuneration, he provided, from cloth which has been woven locally, the wearing apparel of the family. With the growth of villages and towns the tailor set up business in his own premises - often a room in his house - and the habit of travelling the country, which in The Borders was known as 'whipping the cat' fell into desuetude. The first person named 'Maule' who appears in the records of Tulliallan Parish, was a witness to a legal document, in which he is described as a 'taylor' (Note 1). It was his grandson, who, on New Year's Day 1856, opened a small draper's shop in Kincardine's High Street, from which he went on to become the proprietor of one of the largest and most prestigious drapery emporiums in Scotland.

Born in 1832, of humble parentage, Robert Maule, who was named after his father, was an only child. Blessed with a Christian home presided over by a wise, devoted and devout mother, he said in manhood's years, "I owe more to her than I can tell. The memory of her love and prayers prevented me from evil when I was a young apprentice in Glasgow". Poor his parents may have been but they gave him what the Psalmist called, "The heritage of those who fear God's name". That was a legacy he cherished and which guided him in all his affairs throughout his long and highly successful career and which, in turn, he bequeathed to his own son Robert. In boyhood he attended the Tulliallan Parochial School where, under Mr Morgan, he was given a thorough grounding in the three 'Rs'. Of his early years we know of only two incidents, both of which have come down to us from his own lips. One of his regular chores was to go to Blackhall for butter and milk. On going along the footpath, at the side of which a long stretch of grass was growing rather luxuriantly, and it being a wet morning, he stopped to roll up the foot of his trousers and in doing so let fall the shilling he had in his hand. Looking all around he could not find it, so he went on his way ruminating as to what he should do. Would he return home and explain, or go on and seek credit from the farm? As he wandered on, he found a shilling which was certainly NOT the one he had lost, for this one had a mark as if a tacketed boot had tramped upon it. However, it solved his immediate problem and he proceeded in a happier frame of mind, to the farm where he got his order and paid for it with the found shilling. A day or so later, as he was rolling down the legs of his trousers out fell the lost shilling. And that, he said, was the start of my future capital. Country children usually have pet animals. His was a jackdaw. One day, the tame creature flew up the street and perched on the gable of a half-ruined house. Robert followed it. As it seemed to be waiting for him to go up and fetch it, he climbed part of the gable. Seizing hold of a stone which gave way, he tumbled down on to the street followed by a number of loose stones, one of which fell on his head to his severe injury. He was carried home unconscious and it was a week or so before the doctor could assure his parents that he would recover. The mark of the wound remained with him for life. Many years later, when paying a visit to Kincardine, he was told that a good property was in course of erection in Kirk Street. He went to see it and found it was on the site of his accident, and he said to himself: "It will be a few generations before a boy will bring that gable down on his head while looking for a jackdaw".

Leaving school at the age of thirteen, he went to Alva to learn the art of weaving and shawl making, but on the understanding that he would enter eventually upon a mercantile career on which he had set his heart. After two years apprenticeship, he left the factory on 17th May 1846. Forty years later, he recalled the eight-mile walk home on a lovely summer day and how, as he trudged along, he built castles in the air; planning for himself a substantial drapery and manufacturing business, which would bring him considerable prosperity with, of course, no relation to such down-to-earth realities as a draper's shop in Kincardine, in the Tolbooth Wynd in Leith or in Edinburgh's Princes Street, where these boyhood dreams were eventually translated into fact. On reaching Kincardine, the first thing he did was "to run up the loan" to see if his old school was still there. Having returned home, he began his apprenticeship to the drapery trade, in the shop of Mr Donal Buchanan by whom he was engaged for four years at a weekly wage of 2/6, or £6 10s. per annum. The senior apprentice was Charles Alexander, who left two years later to take up a situation in Glasgow, with the result that Robert was promoted to his place. So satisfactorily did he discharge his duties that, a fortnight before the expiry of his apprenticeship, he was invited to remain as salesman, a post hitherto unknown in Mr Buchanan's shop; and he was offered a 600% rise in wages - from 2/6 to 15/- per week.

Naturally he accepted the offer. Next year, Mr Buchanan died and the business was put on the market. It was purchased by the former senior apprentice, Charles Alexander, who now returned to Kincardine. Robert Maule was asked to stay on as salesman, which he did for some months. In arranging the transference of the business, Mrs Buchanan enlisted the assistance of Mr Gentleman, the proprietor of a large drapery business in Falkirk, to assess the value of the stock. On the completion of his assignment, he said to Robert, "if ever you want a change apply to me". Shortly afterwards Robert did that and in 1850 he pitched his moving tent in Falkirk - but not for very long! At the end of three months, he informed his employer that he was leaving for Glasgow, whereupon the following dialogue ensued: "But you were engaged for a year." "I'm going at eleven o'clock today" was the reply. "Well," said the boss, "if you go, you get no salary" . . . to which Robert responded "If so, I go now." There and then, he left - minus his salary! But the tale does not end there. After waiting for thirty- four years he got his salary, and this is how it happened: On Mr Gentleman's death in 1884, when Robert Maule was now a prosperous businessman in Leith, his firm was asked by the trustees of Mr Gentleman's estate, if they would buy up the stock, which was one of the largest in Scotland and valued at £5,000. Robert Maule agreed and sold it on the Falkirk premises. The sale was a huge success and though he had waited long, he claimed that he had got his salary at last - with compound interest added! On going to Glasgow, the eighteen-year-old Kincardine lad went straight to the warehouse of Stewart and McDonald and after an interview with Mr McDonald, the Napoleon of the drapery trade in Scotland in these days, he was accepted and put into the French merino department. That very afternoon he had a row with one of the seniors in a neighbouring section - a not very promising beginning to one's apprenticeship! This is how it happened: A lady customer wanted a certain merino which was on a shelf so high that Robert could not reach it. So he looked round for steps but none were in sight. He then went to the adjacent department which was the linen one and was in the act of removing a pair of steps when the head of the department rushed forward and grabbed them. "You can't take these," he exclaimed, "it's against the rule." But, anxious about his customer, Robert wrenched the steps from him and having served the lady, he immediately replaced the steps. Shortly afterwards the head of the linen department came through to Robert and said: "You did wrong - and don't try it again;" to which he replied defiantly, "If the same circumstances arise tomorrow, I'll do exactly the same - a satisfied customer is what matters most." Thus, Robert revealed that he had a firm hold on one of the cardinal rules of business, that the primary demand is to please one's customers, for without customers no business can survive. But imagine the lad's consternation when one of his colleague's told him that the man whom he had defied was the oldest hand in the warehouse and a great favourite of Mr Stewart the head of the firm: and that they were both Free Church elders in the same congregation. Next morning Mr Mason came round to see Robert and surprisingly was very pleasant. When he asked where he came from and Robert replied "Kincardine-on-Forth", he looked as if an electric shock had passed down his spine, for he too was a Kincardine boy. From that moment, they became good friends and had many talks together, the senior doing all he could to help the newcomer. After a short time, during which he gained much useful experience in Stewart and McDonald's, Robert was invited by Charles Alexander, who had taken over the late Mr Buchanan's drapery business, to return to Kincardine as shop manager; for Mr Alexander had now arranged to go into partnership with a Mr Christie at 82-84 South Bridge, Edinburgh, where together they built up a very successful drapery trade in what was becoming one of the main shopping thoroughfares in Edinburgh. For the next three years Robert Maule was manager of Alexander's drapery store and a right good job he made of it. But he was aware that he never would be satisfied until he had a business of his own. The opportunity eventually came to him. A suitable property, which, for ten years had been occupied by Mr I. Macfarlane, tailor and clothier, as a cloth shop in High Street, became available (Note 2). It adjoined the Commercial Bank. Thus, in The Alloa Advertiser on 29th December 1855, there appeared this advertisement: "New Drapery Establishment in Kincardine. R. Maule will open that very central front shop in the Commercial Bank Buildings on New Year's Day, with an excellent stock of goods of his own personal selection. Further particulars will be given in printed notices". Though there were already several well-stocked draper shops in the town, Maule's, from the word 'go', was a distinct success. In the first year his sales were 50% above his expectations and he was employing two apprentices, David Strong and Alexander Coutts. Although in the mid-decades of the nineteenth century Kincardine was experiencing a period of severe economic depression which lasted for more than half a century, Robert Maule's sales increased year by year - a truly remarkable achievement for a young man. How, one may ask, in so inhospitable an economic climate, did such success attend a new venture, launched by a twenty-four-year- old entrepreneur?

His success can be ascribed partly to his energy, enthusiasm and hard work. As he remarked many years later: "Our Scottish instincts are all for caution but there is also a time to be bold. When one is sure that a certain enterprise has in it the elements of success put all you can, both of your capital and your energy, into it fearlessly." Forty years on, his son said this: "I remember the earlier years of my father's commercial life in Kincardine. No one ever knew the amount of work he put in." In these days there was no closing hour for drapers' shops and it was not until 18th July 1882, that the Kincardine drapers had their first weekly half holiday, by which time Mr Maule had left the town. One day, when he was quite young and was engaged in some ploy, and uncle said, "I think that boy has bees in his bonnet". If he had, they were certainly not drones. All his life he had a tremendous capacity for hard work.

He had, too, a flair for advertising. He knew how to rivet public attention on his place of business - 'Maule's Corner' - he called it. At a time when there were no professional advertising agencies and every man had to write his own script, he appreciated the value of an opening phrase which was an eye-catcher; and the crisp, compelling headline which would induce the most desultory reader, who was only scanning the advertisements, to pause and read on. In 1884, his son, Robert, who had been his father's apprentice thirty years previously, still remembered some of the advertisements of those early days, and, in a speech, quoted one which began:

"Amidst the cry all around of dull trade, there is always a stir at The Commercial Buildings . . .".

There was this also, he went personally not only to the warehouses in nearby Glasgow, as the other merchants did also, but to the factories in London, in Manchester and in the surrounding districts - as he never hesitated to make clear in his advertisement - to purchase at factory prices, the best goods available and he was content with moderate profits. Robert Maule was always prepared to travel the second mile, if by so doing, he could serve better the interests of his customers.

Behind and directing all his activities there was this: He was a young man of unimpeachable integrity. Honesty was his policy. As he put it in later years, "the true basis of all business relationships is that those with whom we have dealings should have faith in us and that we should always strive not to betray, but to merit such faith."

By this time he was married (Note 3). His wife was a Kincardine girl - Charlotte Rankin. Theirs was an ideal partnership in which she gave him the secure base of a happy home. She was unfailing in her support, and when the going was hard she was never lacking in the encouragement she provided. There first house was the upper flat of a two-storey block in Toll Road rented from Captain Simpson (Note 4).

Robert Maule's first sizeable contract as a Kincardine draper came to him a few months after he had set up in business. In June of that year a subscription had been organised in the town to provide a uniform for the members of the local instrumental band, some fifteen in number. A specimen suit was designed. The material was to be a superfine navy cloth, trimmed with scarlet. The cap was to be of blue and scarlet cloth trimmed with a thistle and a bugle at the front. The belt was to be leather with an attractive buckle bearing a representation of the king of the forest. Offers were called for from the local merchants. Robert Maule secured the contract. The Clackmannanshire Advertiser made this comment on the uniform which he had provided: "Mr Maule appears to be anxious to fulfil his bargain in the most honourable manner, as the style in which it is got up displays great taste, good workmanship and an excellent fit, all of which combined, are calculated to be a high recommendation to one commencing, such as he is." Backed by skill and integrity, his business kept growing in a community where there was a steadily diminishing population and decreasing wealth, until by 1861 he was forced either to look for larger premises or have his present shop extended. The Commercial Bank occupied the two rooms immediately to the rear of his shop, so he proposed to his landlady, Miss Archibald, that the banker, Mr A. C. Stephen, who combined with that role a legal practice and the town clerkship of Culross, should be allocated two rooms beyond the ones he presently occupied and so allow the drapery shop to be extended into the bank's accommodation. The banker's private house was above both the bank and Mr Maule's shop. When he was acquainted with the young draper's proposal Mr Stephen acquired other accommodation and on his removal, Robert Maule obtained possession both of the office which Mr Stephen had occupied and the house also. Now, he was able to accommodate to advantage two new lines which he had introduced in 1859 and 1860 - "Suits made

up at the shortest notice by tailors of undoubted experience";
and, "ready made gents dress and tweed suits" (Note 5) - the
latter being a quite new departure in the trade. The necessary
alterations to the property were preceded by - "A Great
Popular Sale" to be conducted daily, with the shop remaining
open till 9 p.m. In due course, there appeared another
advertisement - "The Object Accomplished"; and the public
were informed that, "it has now become a household word
that all the year round at Maule's everybody receives
attention, courtesy and a large choice of first class goods at
strictly moderate prices".

Almost simultaneously with enlarging his premises in
Kincardine, his energy was finding another outlet. This was a
partnership into which he entered with Fleming Bowie, when
on Thursday, 19th April, 1860 they opened a shop in High
Street, Dollar where they proposed to carry on a first class
family trade, "Mr Maule having just returned from the
manufacturing districts with a large selection of good".
Anticipating success, as he always did, they advertised also
for two assistants - "respectable lads" - who were bidden to
apply to Mr Maule. The business in Dollar prospered
mightily. Within a few months they were seeking "a milliner
of undoubted ability, experience and good taste" and in
October, six months after having commenced trading, they
spoke of "the very liberal encouragement" given by the public
in Dollar. So much was this the case, that as in Kincardine,
they had to extend their premises, a process which was
preceded by "a grand sale of their entire stock at bargain
prices no less than 25% to 30% under market value". Only a
month later, there appeared, surprisingly against such a

background, a notice of dissolution of partnership by mutual consent; Mr Bowie engaging to receive all monies due to the firm and consenting to discharge all their debts. It was made clear that he would continue the business as sole partner which he did successfully for a number of years. The reason for this unexpected development is not hard to find. Robert Maule's business in Kincardine was growing fast and with his enlarged premises it would develop still further. Moreover, it was entirely his own property and though he never feared to take well calculated risks, he was not one to allow his resources in energy or in cash to be overstretched. So with his partner being left with a viable business in Dollar, he pulled out honourably, in order to concentrate on and diversify his interests in Kincardine. In August 1862 we find him advertising for good shawl weavers as he intended to commence, in premises in the Wester Quarter of Kincardine, the manufacture of "shawls of every texture, size and shade" along with shirting: a dual industry which he continued for several years after he had disposed of his drapery in Kincardine.

Shortly after midnight on Tuesday, 14th May 1867, a disastrous fire broke out at the triple mills owned by Mr William Young of Muirhead and as the town had no fire engine the flour and meal mills became a total loss. Nothing remained but "rent and blackened walls". Only the barley mill was saved. The loss was estimated at £1,000, a large sum in these days. By the beginning of the New Year Mr Maule had purchased the burnt out premises and had had them converted into a weaving factory, thus enlarging his Mercer Street properties and adding to the manufacture of shawls and shirtings, that of tweeds, tartan plaids, and blankets; the complex becoming known as "The Viewforth Factory" (Note 6).

In the spring of 1863 the Prince of Wales, later to become King Edward VII, married the Danish Princess Alexandra. Kincardine played its small part in the National celebrations. Flags were flying on many houses from Tulliallan Castle to the humblest cottage. 160 baskets of groceries were distributed to the poorest citizens. The wedding day was a local holiday. Church bells rang out a merry peal from noon to 1 p.m. - the exact time of the marriage service. There was a Royal Salute from the shipyard of Messrs Duncan Wright and a dinner in the Commercial Hotel at 4 p.m., for the town's leading citizens. All week, the shops had been decorated but none so lavishly as Robert Maule's. It stole the show. House and shop were draped in red and white cloth interspersed with padella (Note 7) and gas illuminations. The young draper had put much through into his display and part of his reward lay in the publicity which it engendered, for, we are told, "crowds congregated to see the illuminations which were quite novel for Kincardine". The day's festivities ended with a torchlight procession by the youth of the town and a huge bonfire at the pier head. Robert Maule's final commercial undertaking in Kincardine is as adventurous as it is surprising. In July 1868 he bought the barque Lord Byron of Glasgow, a vessel of 650 tons, for the North American trade. She was put under the command of Captain William Gibb, but how the experiment fared we are not told. That it took place, however, is added testimony to the fact that this young Kincardine man had the spirit of the true entrepreneur, who does not shy away from commercial challenges but welcomes them and indeed, creates them as fresh opportunities on which to build success.

With so much on his plate he had little time for recreation. When he resided at Toll Road, gardening was his hobby and at the Horticultural Show in the Parochial Schoolroom in 1857 he won a prize for "his exhibit of large peas". For a short period he served on The Parochial Board, but he took little part in public affairs which in Kincardine were vitiated by bitterness and spite. At a meeting on 6th June 1868, when the topic under discussion was whether Kincardine should abide in Perthshire or go into Clackmannanshire he spoke in favour of the transference; but such was "the noisiness of the audience" that he had to leave his speech unfinished. He was keenly interested in The Glasgow- Kincardine Society, was frequently a member of the platform party at its annual soiree, and seldom returned home without a substantial donation from the exiles for the poor of their native town.

Like his parents he was a member of the United Presbyterian Congregation (Note 8) but his earliest known activity did not make him very popular! Mr Donald Buchanan, with whom he served his apprenticeship, was convener of the seat letting committee. One Saturday evening, a member of the congregation came into the shop complaining that though he had paid his seat rent his name was not on the pew. Robert was sent to rectify the mistake and when he arrived at the church, William, the beadle, was just beginning to ring the eight o'clock bell. He gave the rope to Robert and told him to continue ringing while he went for a light. Robert, who was keen to do the job well, rang so vigorously that he broke the iron rod to which the bell was attached and the noisy tongue lapsed into silence. In consternation, he ran back to the shop, to tell Mr Buchanan what had happened and he, with his tongue in his cheek, told Robert that he would have to appear before the Kirk Session and would have to pay for repairing the damage. The former did not trouble him but he was greatly worried about the latter, for he did not have that sort of money. However, the bell was repaired and nothing was said. "But," he added, "I will never forget the sensation in the town next day. The family clocks were charged with unsteadiness. People looked solemnly at each other and gravely enquired - 'have you heard the bell?' 'What's wrang wi' the bell?' and some even asked 'Is this the Sabbath?' . . . Sequel - I never meddled with a church bell again!"

His first adult intervention in the affairs of the congregation was in 1863 during a prolonged vacancy, the filling of which gave rise to serious dissension. So bitter did it become, that Mr Stephen, a lawyer and banker, told the congregation meeting bluntly, on 3rd October, that he had left the squabbling Free Church "to get peace and quiet but had found nothing but bickering and brawling". That proved a salutary rebuke and it led Robert Maule, to whom bitterness was equally displeasing, to move at the next congregational meeting, a fortnight later, that they get on with the job of selecting a minister and put forward a name to the Presbytery. Thereupon Mr Welch was nominated and all but unanimously supported (Note 9). A year later, Robert Maule was chosen by the congregation as one of six new elders who were ordained on 4th December 1864 and in March 1868 he was appointed to represent the congregation at the Presbytery. He was as assiduous in his discharge of these responsibilities as he was in his business affairs for to him duty was a stern voice which always demanded obedience.

During the Kincardine years, he lived much under fortune's smile. He had a happy home and loyal, supportive wife. In business he had the Midas touch. But he had known fortune's frown as well. There had been sadness in his family life. No fewer than three of his children died when very young - Jane, on her first birthday; James, when he was only sixteen months and Lizzie Ann, two days after James. Meantime, his son, Robert, who had been born in 1852, was on the verge of manhood's estate and to him we now must turn.

Of his boyhood years, the story of only one incident has come down to us. In July 1863, when he was eleven years of age, he was engaged, along with some companions, swinging on a rope tied to the branch of a tree when he either lost his hold or the rope broke, "whereby he was precipitated to the ground and received severe injuries". He was quite seriously ill for some time but made a complete recovery. He obtained his earliest schooling in the local parochial school under the headmastership of Thomas Buchanan (Note 10) to whom, on his retirement, Robert paid a well merited tribute when he replied to the toast of "Mr Buchanan's former pupils", at a complimentary dinner to their old teacher in The Ship Inn, Leith, when he was presented with a handsome silver tray costing £55. From the school in Kincardine, Robert moved to Dollar Academy, where he was a good average pupil: and in 1867, when in the upper division of class IV, he won the first prize for mental arithmetic. He was much liked, we are told, by his teachers and fellow pupils for he had an outgoing, open, generous nature and a pleasing sense of humour.

On leaving school, he joined his father as an apprentice in the Kincardine draper shop, where, under a most exacting boss, he was given a thorough training in the trade. His pay was small, and at the conclusion of his apprenticeship no increase was forthcoming. So, to alert his father to the need for a rise in wages, he adopted a clever stratagem. He applied for a situation, advertised in The Scotsman by a well-known Edinburgh firm, but not in the drapery line. After some correspondence, he was offered the job and with the letter in his hand he went to the head of the house and said: "Now, can you do better for me than this?" The trick succeeded. His services were retained at an increased wage. Baptised by Dr Gardiner, the minister of the United Presbyterian Church, Robert was a regular attender at the Sunday School and, sixty years later, recalled Dr Gardiner coming in each Sunday to open their meeting with prayer. Before Robert was ten, Dr Gardiner left Kincardine to go to the Dean Church in Edinburgh and at the age of eleven Robert signed the Call to Dr Gardiner's successor as an 'adherent'. In these days the church had no organisation specifically for teenager but a branch of the Young Men's Christian Association was formed in 1868, and from its inception Robert was a keen member. He was appointed secretary and at their first soiree and business meeting, "he gave", we are told, "an able and eloquent introductory speech". In 1871 he gave an address on "Our choice of Companions" which was described as "very clear and instructive". To an audience of sixty that night in The Reading Room, which had been specially decorated for the occasion, he submitted his last report as Secretary, "which" it was said, "had been got up with marked care and ability". He referred to the many difficulties "in our decreasing town where our young men are drafted off in numbers each year", in spite of which the attendance at their meetings had been encouraging. After a sumptuous tea, there was singing and music, Robert's sister Christine "playing some fine pieces on the piano". At the end, Robert proposed a vote of thanks to the lady tea maker. The Y.M.C.A.   was a strong, lively society and Robert Maule one of its most active members. His other interests were curling, of which he remained a life-long devotee, and cricket.

The steady decline in Kincardine's population and its poor economic prospects made Robert Maule, a young man of energy and ambition, ill at ease in a business which was devoid of any hope of further growth (Note 11). So, as his father confessed, "it was largely at his urging that I began to look out for what in the church, ministers call 'a larger sphere of usefulness'." The opportunity arose in the autumn of 1872, when the bankrupt stock of Mr John Ord, a draper in Leith, came on the market. At the auction, bidding was brisk, for Leith was a prosperous and expanding sea port. The initial bid, proposed by the auctioneer, was 20/- per £. Mr Maule's first offer was 20s.6d . . . and the price rose rapidly at one penny per pound, until it was finally won by Mr Maule for 21s. 2d. per pound; making a total of £5,352 17s. 10d. for stock which had been valued at £5,000. It was the highest price paid for a drapery store in Scotland to date. Having secured the business and a lease of the property Mr Maule returned home with, in his pocket, a proof copy of next morning's Scotsman, announcing that the business in Tolbooth Wynd, Leith, had been acquired by Robert Maule and Son. As yet, Robert had no idea that he had been taken into partnership. The reading of it came as a shock to him and crossing the room he shook his father by the hand and said: "I'll do my best" - and he certainly did! Speaking a quarter of a century later about their partnership the son said: "Partnership is too cold a word to use of our association. It has been one of the most glorious unions that could ever exist between two men. It was an alliance formed for business purposes but based on a bond of affection the strongest, I think, that ever existed between a father and a son". Their first task was to get rid of the bankrupt's stock, which they did at a "Great Clearance Sale" (Note 12), Mr Maule adding, as a special inducement to the public, "a few hundred tartan plaids from our looms at Kincardine". In their first year in Leith, their trade was doubled and when they finally gave up, they were doing four times as much as in their opening year. In Kincardine, the news that Mr Maule was to leave the town was greeted with universal regret. But before he left in the spring of 1873, he was entertained, in March to what was described as "a superb banquet" in the Commercial Hotel, at which over 50 gentlemen were present. Mr Buchanan, the schoolmaster, presided and Mr. David Norrie, a native of Kincardine and now postmaster at Alloa, was croupier. Tributes were paid to the guest who, out of his 41 1/2 years of life had been not more than two years absent from his native town and who for 16 years had conducted a highly successful business. Good wishes were extended to him for the success of his new venture as also to Mr Strong who had taken over the Kincardine shop. Thanking his hosts for the honour accorded to him that night, Mr Maule alluded to the new name of the firm. Of his partner, he was glad to say that "for years he had acted his part well and had done his utmost to merit my approval". At the close of the function, Mr Maule gave five guineas to the most necessitous families in the town, so that they might share in the pleasure he had enjoyed that night. This was characteristic of him - as it was to be also of his son - that when there was in their family circle an occasion for rejoicing, the poorest in the community should be given reason to be glad. Though he terminated his drapery business in Kincardine that year, he continued the manufacture of shawls, cotton shirtings, tweeds, tartan plaids, blankets and handkerchiefs for several years.

In Leith, prosperity marked him for her own. The recurring sales of bankrupt stock as also the seasonal sales of fashion goods, made a widespread appeal and day after day the shop was overcrowded. On commencing business at Tolbooth Wynd the firm employed 40 hands, ten years later there were over 100 on the payroll. Within two years they bought out the lease of the property and the ground and buildings to the rear, for over £7,000, in order to increase floorage and to improve the facilities for staff and customers. And here, let it be said, that the relationship between employers and employees could not have been bettered and to cement that congenial relationship, Mr Maule and Robert entertained their entire staff annually at a dinner and dance. Speaking, years later, of Mr Maule as a Master, James Taylor (Note 13) who had been long in his service, said: "He was all that any servant could wish for; in all these years I never heard him speak an angry word". Their enlarged premises soon proved inadequate for their ever-increasing trade. Further extensions became imperative. So, in 1888, they erected new buildings double the size of the original, fronting Tolbooth Wynd and Henderson Street, with large saloons which made Maule's one of the handsomest and most convenient drapery establishments in any town or city in Scotland, not excepting Edinburgh and Glasgow.

When, in 1873, he closed his shop door in Kincardine for the last time, Mr Maule was by no means done with his native town.

Take his business interests: In his speech at the complimentary dinner to Mr Maule, Mr Mustard spoke of "the torpor and decline of business in the town reflected in the sequestration of several traders". One of the unfortunates was to be Mr Strong - Mr Maule's successor. On March 10th 1877, a notice appeared in the local paper, announcing a "Great winding up sale at the Famous Old Corner", which went on to inform the public that Messrs Maule had purchased the entire stock of Mr David Strong for over £1,000 and were to offer unprecedented bargains to the people of Kincardine. The sale went on for several weeks to the great benefit of the community. At the same time Messers Maule disposed of their factories in Kincardine and Alva - "The handsome woollen factory, Viewforth, Kincardine, including plant and 17 looms all in working order. Viewforth factory was rebuilt by the proprietor and has attached a two storey dwelling house and stabling - entry to be given at Whitsunday 1877".

Take his holidays: Without fail, Mr and Mrs Maule spent their annual vacation in their native town where for some years they leased Kincardine House and later Burnbrae; until 1893, when, at the termination of the lease, he disposed of much of the furnishing by public auction. In Kincardine he loved to move unobtrusively among the local people with, as one citizen remarked, "a kind word for everybody and many a long chat with the companions of his boyhood and youth".

Take his church connection: It was renewed annually during his holiday residence in the town and also in January, when he and his wife attended the congregational soiree. During the ministry of the Rev. John Macfarlane a tower was added, in 1832, to the original plain and characterless building. During the last week of December 1883, Thomas Mitchell, a local builder, began dismantling the roof of the tower in order to replace it with a new and more elegant one, "to be embellished by a turret clock with four dials". Congratulating the U.P. congregation on receiving so handsome a gift, the Alloa Advertiser added that, "standing about the middle of the town the clock will be a conspicuous object from all points, and we sincerely hope that it will be illumined in the winter months". To mark their appreciation of so generous a gift, the Kirk Session entertained Mr Maule to dinner in the Commercial Hotel, on Monday 28th January, at which 60 gentlemen were present. Proposing the health of their guest, Rev. Mr Munro spoke of how every summer finds him spending his too short holiday with us. "The clock," he added, "is an ornament to the tower roof and the tower roof an ornament to the clock and both are an ornament to the church." In his reply, Mr Maule said that during his holiday the previous year, he had heard the desirability of a clock often spoken about and on consulting his adviser over many years, he realised that he would have her full support if he should resolve to present a clock to the church". At the close of his speech he handed to Mr Muncro a cheque to pay the entire cost of its erection, £171, he having already paid the clock makers, Messrs R. H. Miller of Edinburgh. Responding to the toast of the firm, "Robert Maule and Son", Robert said: "I have known my father all my life and great as is the honour conferred on him today, I can say that he well deserves it all: for I have never known him withhold help from the needy or from any deserving cause." As their custom was, Mr and Mrs Maule attended the congregational soiree that night and when called upon to address the gathering, he assured them that he would have been much happier sitting in his pew than standing on the platform.

At the congregational soiree a year later, Mr Munro intimated another generous gift to the church. "Mr Maule," he said, "had gifted the property south of the church, consisting of a two storied house, a one storey house adjoining, and a small plot of ground (Note 14), all nicely lying into the church property, so that there now belonged to them the whole of the triangular piece of ground in the middle of the town. The purpose for which Mr Maule had transferred the ground to them was for the erection of a hall and suite of rooms, for a library, Session meetings etc. Mr Baldie, architect of the tower roof, was drawing up plans and the building committee intended, with the consent of the congregation, to build a hall to accommodate 300-350 people: so that, besides being useful for the congregation, it might be useful for the town also." Mr Munro then remarked that "the tower was built in 1832, the year of the great Reform Bill, and with the passing of the third

Reform Bill in 1884, the year when the clock was erected, they had in the tower and the clock, two erections connected with great historical events in their nation's political history." By December 1886 the new hall (Note 15) was, as one of the local newspapers reports: "ready, amid great rejoicings, to be opened on Monday 20th". Mr Maule, who presided, expressed his hesitation in accepting the invitation given to him; on two counts: he regarded himself as the wrong person to make the principal speech and he knew that the available funds were as yet insufficient to cover the whole cost. As to the second, he was now glad to say that the Treasurer was in funds and the hall would be opened free of debt." In thanking the donors within and without the congregation, Rev. Mr Munro said that among the outside contributors, Mr Maule Jr was the most liberal. The cost of the hall was £570. That morning the Treasurer had £470. Later in the day Mr Maule had handed to the Treasurer a cheque for £100, thus ensuring that the hall would be opened free of debt. "The hall, like the clock," said Mr Munro, "belongs to the congregation and will, like the clock, be used for the public good." Following the opening ceremony there was a musical programme and during the proceedings, which did not end until 11 p.m., one of the speakers was Rev. Dr Gardiner who had been one of the earliest ministers of the church (Note 16).

Though this may anticipate events chronologically, it is convenient to mention here, further generous gifts from the Maule family to the Kincardine U.P. Church. On 11th July 1904, the Kirk Session received a letter from Robert Maule asking them to accept from himself the gift of a Listz organ, "which he trusted would be helpful in the praise part of the

Service", and saying that he would be pleased to pay also "for the cost of the improved ventilation of the hall". At the same meeting the Kirk Session expressed thanks to Mrs Dewar and Mrs Stevenson, daughters of the late Mr Maule, who had paid for "a new platform for the church". Never was a church in Kincardine dealt with so generously by its former members as was the United Presbyterian Church by the Maule family.

Take his benevolence: Every year at Hogmanay Mr Maule gave a basket of groceries to 80 or more of the poorest citizens in Kincardine, the provision being supplied by local grocers and distributed without regard to church affiliation. In days when there was, locally, great animosity between the churches, he made human need the sole criterion of his charity. So most of his gifts went to members of the Established Church of which he had never been a member. He was as shrewd in his benevolence as he was in his business. He ensured that his provision went to the "virtuous poor". He was not one to subsidise the lazy or the waster. On occasions of special rejoicing in his family circle this good man made opportunity to bring cheer into the homes of the poorest. In 1881 when Robert, married, he gave £12 to be distributed to the needy. In 1882 on the occasion of his daughter, Christine's marriage, he gave a basket of groceries to 75 families; as he did again in 1887, when his second daughter, Catherine Jane, was married. And, in May 1896, when he himself celebrated his jubilee as a businessman, he remembered the poor in his native town in like manner. No wonder when one invalid received her gift, she exclaimed: "Mr Maule should live for ever: he's so kind to us poor". He made sure that his kindness would outlive him. In his will, he bequeathed £100 to the Kirk

Session of the United Presbyterian Church to enable them to continue his benevolence for a further five years; at the end of which his son, Robert, took over his father's role and so, between them, the poorest citizens of their native town received hogmanay gifts for forty-one years.

On the domestic front, life for Mr Maule had gone on in the even tenor of its way. Now, a prosperous businessman, he had purchased a desirable residence in what was then the village of Corstorphine, three miles to the west of Edinburgh. His family had married, Robert in 1881 to Miss Janet McIntosh, the daughter of a Leith contractor; Christine his elder daughter to John Dewar, a merchant of Leith; and his youngest daughter, Catherine Jane, to James St Clair Stevenson, an Edinburgh Merchant.

In November 1890, the Maules made the most ambitious venture of their career when they bought the property 146-149 Princes Street. It had, previous to 1879, been the Osbourne Hotel, but a disastrous fire in that year had left it a blackened shell. The site was bought by The Liberal Party. After being rebuilt, it was opened in 1880 as The Liberal Club by Mr Gladstone, who was M.P. for Midlothian. The new building was a handsome structure and the site ideal for the purpose Mr Maule intended. At a juncture where more streets converge than anywhere else in Edinburgh, within easy reach for high class trade from the West End, well placed for the middle class trade from Lothian Road and beyond, being opposite the Caledonian Railway Station where passengers from the villages and towns of West Lothian, Stirlingshire, Fife and Dundee alighted, it had a strategic position for trading. The purchase price was £41,500, a very large sum in these days.

The move surprised many of Mr Maule's friends. Some feared he had bitten off more than he could chew. To them, he replied that "there were more worlds to conquer".

Figure 5: Princes Street, the West End, showing the premises of Robert Maule and son, 1900

Others, out of envy, would not have grieved if it had brought about his downfall. But Robert Maule was no reckless speculator. He was a canny Scot. He and Robert had read the signs of the times. Princes Street was changing from being a residential street to becoming a business and commercial thoroughfare. Edinburgh was expanding westwards. Leith had reached its zenith in prosperity. If a business was to have prospects of growth it would have to be located in Edinburgh and the likeliest growth point was towards the west. If Robert and his father had any consolation in leaving Leith it was that their business was to be continued by Taylor Mearns and Co., and that Mr Taylor was a Kincardine man. For the change of use from club to shop, the Princes Street property required major reconstruction. The de- tailed logistics of planning adequate supplies and sufficient staff for the various departments presented a formidable challenge.

But the two men at the top were of high intellectual calibre. For nine months, the building was in the hands of contractors. Buyers were sent to the principal markets in Europe, in quest of new fashions and novelties, which would be on display in Edinburgh for the first time. The business of Carlisle and Watts in Princes Street, of which Messrs Maule had been the owners for several years, was incorporated in the new premises. They were dealers in high class leather goods, in heraldic stationery and were manufacturers of dressing cases for which The Royal Warrant "By Appointment to the Queen" had been granted. By 4th February 1894, Saint Valentine's Day, every department was fully equipped and staffed with about 300 employees ready for the opening hour, 10 a.m. The sale that day was a stunning success. In The Scotsman, two days later, a notice appeared expressing the firm's gratitude to the public for the patronage accorded to them. It went on to say: "The numbers visiting the warehouse yesterday were at certain hours appalling and we believe the amount of business done for the day stands unparalleled in the trade". They apologised to the many who had to leave the shop unserved, but the influx of customers had far exceeded anticipation. The opening day's experience was no flash in the pan. Trade kept expanding. Adjacent properties were purchased as they came on the market and, in 1897, they carried out a huge extension which brought them round the corner - Maule's Corner - reminiscent of the Kincardine Shop's location - into Hope Street. What the Maules had created was not just one more large emporium. It was a revolution in shopping; where, in six floors containing almost everything a family required, the prime consideration was the comfort and convenience of the customer. Theirs was the first store in Edinburgh to have electric lifts, manned by attendants, to all six floors and the basement.

Theirs was the first store to incorporate a luncheon room and tea room for which all the edibles were prepared by a highly skilled staff, in model kitchens, which were open to customers' inspection at all hours. Theirs was the first store to provide a coffee room for gentlemen with lounge chairs, where "coffee that was better than the best cocktail" could be enjoyed and where all the facilities of a private club, including a smoking room, were available without having to pay a membership fee. Theirs was the first store to have a lounge, where customers could rest in comfortable easy chairs, read newspapers and magazines supplied by the firm, write letters on writing tables provided, and even post them! In the beautifully laid out Palm Court there was always an enticing display of chocolates and confectionery, and a large notice - "A concession unique in Edinburgh! We pay postage on all sweets". To shop at Maule's was not to engage in one more buying expedition. It was, as the proprietors meant it to be, "a new and pleasant experience". The catchy phrase - "Meet me at Maule's" - very quickly became a household word (Note 17).

The story of the Princes Street enterprise was a re-run on a much larger scale, of the success stories of Leith and Kincardine, based not only on "the flair for business" which father and son had, on their capacity for hard work, their consideration for the convenience of their customers and the courtesy of their staff, but on the known integrity of both partners which in the commercial world made 'Maules' a synonym for honesty. Mr Maule died at his home, The Lea, Corstorphine, in March 1901 having been predeceased by his wife ten years previously. Tributes were paid to him in both the national and provincial newspapers. But nowhere was the news of his death received with greater sorrow than it was in his native Kincardine, where there had been not only legitimate pride in his outstandingly prosperous mercantile career but where there were recalled his many "deeds of kindness and of love" which had won for him the respect of all classes and the gratitude of the poorest.

In his will, he left his shares in the business with the entire stock and fittings to Robert; with the option of buying the heritable property. The remainder of his estate, after a few private legacies, was divided equally among his family. Thus in 1901, Robert became the sole proprietor of the business.

With trade maintaining its momentum, the business running as smoothly as a well-tuned engine and a loyal staff attending to its day to day efficiency, he was now able to take a more active part in public affairs. A Liberal in politics and chairman of The Scottish Reform Club and of the Executive of the

Scottish Liberal Association, he was a close friend of Mr Asquith the Prime Minister, to whom he gave hospitality on his visits to Edinburgh. More than once, he was invited to stand for Parliament. Safe seats were offered to him. But he opted for philanthropic work. For many years he was chairman of The Courant Fund (Note 18), whose object was to provide the city's poorest children with a day's outing to the country. When, during the war and in the post-war years, the cost of the excursions outran the resources of the Fund, it was Robert Maule's personal generosity that enabled them to be continued. He frequently entertained handicapped children to a garden party at his home, 'Ashbrook, Ferry Road. As many as 200 children, as in 1924, were brought on a summer afternoon in cabs. They were served with a picnic tea in the garden, played suitable games, were entertained by a concert party and on leaving, each child was provided with a toy and sweets.

Following the practice of his father in the Leith days he provided annually a dinner dance for his employees in The Assembly Rooms in George Street, where some 300 were his guests for the evening. In reply to the toast of his health, he invariably reviewed the events of the previous year. His speech in 1913 is one of more than ordinary interest. Recalling that 1911 had been the Coronation Year of King George V and Queen Mary, with their State visit to Edinburgh, he reminded his audience that it had been a bumper year for trade; but what was more pleasing was that the record had been kept up in 1912. Then followed an announcement which gave pleasure to all. He said that he had now taken his son Robert - Robert the Third - into partnership. The health of the new partner, who was a graduate of Christ's College, Cambridge and who had thereafter learned all aspects of the trade at various centres, was pledged enthusiastically. Responding to the toast, Robert said it would be his endeavour to continue the high traditions of the past and especially to cultivate "the deep and abiding interest which his father and grandfather had always had in the welfare of their fellow workers". Here, may it be added, that not a few employees who showed artistic talent, musical or otherwise, had been provided with special training for the improvement of their gifts, by Mr Maule. A Justice of the Peace for the City of Edinburgh since 1902, he was also a Director of the Edinburgh Tramways Corporation, a Trustee of the Edinburgh Savings Bank and an active vice-president of the Edinburgh Young Men's Christian Association, and of the Commercial Travellers' Christian Union. Like his father he was blessed with a happy marriage, where his partner took an active interest in the welfare of their employees with whom she was most popular. The family circle consisted of two daughters and Robert - the elder being married to Mr Joseph Scott of Congleton, Drem, and the younger to Captain Walker, Scarborough. In 1903 he acquired a small estate in the Breadalbane country at Tummel Bridge, where he built a house modelled on the plan of a Swiss chalet, which he named Daleroch Lodge (Note 19). There, he had ample opportunity to indulge in two of his favourite pastimes, angling and curling, and he became President of the local curling club.

The year 1913 saw him reach the zenith of his career when, in The Birthday Honours List, he was awarded a knighthood. Addressing, some months later, the annual general meeting of the Glasgow-Kincardine Association, an occasion which Sir Robert - as we now must call him - never failed to attend, Rev. John McLaren, who was that year's President, said that "if the Kincardine people had had their way, Sir Robert Maule would have been knighted long ago. They only wondered why the King had been so remiss as to have waited so long." Following his father's practice, this knightly benefactor added that year to his hogmanay gift of a well-stocked basket of groceries to the poor in Kincardine, a supply of coal so that they too would have special reason to rejoice. The Royal honour bestowed upon Sir Robert gave his friends a chance to show him their esteem and affection. In July, he was entertained to a complimentary dinner by the Scottish Reform Club and the Scottish Liberal Club, at which more than 100 gentlemen attended. *(continued below)*

IMAGE DESCRIPTION: On the opposite page is Messrs Maule's emporium dressed over all on the occasion of the State Visit of King Edward VII and Queen Alexandra to Edinburgh. Their premises were decorated even more elaborately for the State Visit of King George V and Queen Mary in July 1911, and in the opinion of both the general public and of those most competent to judge the palm for the best decorated building in the city went to Robert Maule and Son. The entire property was swathed in foliage of various hues interspersed by blooms of many colours. Prominently displayed on the facade was a medallion of King George with the crown superimposed and the letters G and M on each side while on the topmost point floated the Lion Rampant of Scotland. At night "the blazing splendour of countless electric lamps revealed the beauty of the building and the decorative scheme to the intense gratification of the surging crowds who came in their thousands every night to see it". For a succession of afternoons Herr Meny and his White Viennese Band, one of Vienna's most celebrated orchestras, played a variety of popular tunes in the store and in the evenings on the balcony outside.

The firm of Sir Robert Maule and Son also carried out with marked success the decoration of all the city's official buildings. The decorations of the Palace of Holyrood and the construction and furnishing of three substantial pavilions for the King's guests as well as the arrangements for the Royal Garden Party were entrusted to Maule's. It may be added that the firm was annually engaged for many years to supplement the rather sparse furnishings of Holyrood Palace for the visit and residence of the Lord High Commissioner to the General

Assembly of the Church of Scotland. True to his character Sir Robert, on the occasion of the Royal visit, saw to it that many households in the poorer districts of the city were supplied with flags gratis so that none should feel that they were not having a share in Edinburgh's welcome to their King and Queen.

(continued from above)

The health of the Chief Guest was proposed by the Solicitor General. In the course of an eloquent reply, Sir Robert said that his politics began in Kincardine where he was fed on Liberalism by his father. Together they had worked for the return of the Liberal candidates, Sir Robert Adam, who had held the seat for twenty years. In Leith he had actively done the same and he was doing the same now at Tummel Bridge. He concluded an able address by extolling the achievements of the Liberal Governments under Sir Henry Campbell-Bannerman and Mr Asquith.

Thus far, the sun of prosperity had shone brightly on Sir Robert out of a cloudless sky. With the advent of 1914, shadows deep were to cross his pathway. Scarcely had the year begun, when Lady Maule, who had been ill for some months, died. August 4th, 1914, will ever be remembered as the date on which Britain went to war with Germany. Within a few weeks Captain Walker, his younger daughter's husband, was killed. Shortly thereafter his nephew, Lieutenant Dewar, died in battle. Heavy as these blows were, the severest of the hammer blows of fate, descended on Sir Robert in June 1915, when he received the news that his son, Robert, had been killed in the Dardanelles Campaign on 29th May. If anything could have increased the severity of that blow, it was that, along with the War Office telegram, a letter from Robert was delivered, saying that after having been on special duty as part of the escort for Sir Ian Hamilton, the Commander- in-Chief, he had rejoined his regiment where he wished to be. Three such blows would have felled most men; but with the resilience which his Christian Faith gave him, Sir Robert bore a brave face in public. Like the King of Israel he wore "his sackcloth within" (Note 20).

In November, following his wife's death, he attended The Glasgow- Kincardine Annual Soiree where, in the presence of 400 members, he received an illuminated address in appreciation of his support of the Association over many years, during the last seven of which he had been the Honorary President, and to show their pleasure at his having been honoured by the King.

Early in 1915 he had received from a young officer on the Western Front a letter, relating how in a captured German trench, he had picked up a page from the Dollar Academy Magazine, which carried a short article about Sir Robert Maule, complete with a photograph: and beside it, another page with a poem, "The Call of Spring". How it was in a German trench no one can understand. But more remarkable, is the fact that the soldier who had picked it up was a former pupil of Dollar Academy, now a gunner with the British Expeditionary Force; and that he was Fred Munro, the eldest son of the Rev. Robert Munro, who was minister of

Kincardine U.P. Church when Robert Maule was a young man.

After being seven years a widower Sir Robert re-married in 1921. The marriage took place in St Columba's Church, London. The bride was a daughter of Mr Lawrence Drysdale, Manor Steps, Alloa and the widow of Mr John Fyfe, Chief Government Valuer for Scotland. This marriage too was a happy one. His second wife shared his interest in the welfare of his employees and his philanthropic concern for the disadvantaged. Once more, his friends showed their affection. His Princes Street employees and those at Dalreoch gave him and Lady Maule valuable gifts as did the members of the Maule, the Nothern Maule and Edinburgh Winter Bowling Association at a banquet in the Victoria Hall.

On 5th February 1921 the Tulliallan Curling Club held their annual supper in the Commercial Hotel, to which Sir Robert Maule motored through, as it coincided with the fiftieth anniversary of his having joined the club. In his speech, he recalled that some years previously, he had presented a couple of curling stones for competition. These had been won by David Bowie. That night he offered another pair for a similar competition. A fortnight later, by Sir Robert's invitation, four members of the club, with David Bowie as skip, played a friendly game against Sir Robert and three members of the Waverly Club on Haymarket Ice Rink. It was a well contested game. After three hours play, the result was Tulliallan 12, Waverly 14. The entire company then motored to the Caledonian Hotel for lunch, provided by their host. For the visitors, it was an occasion to remember which was often recalled in later years.

In the nineteenth century, due largely to the enthusiasm of one of the Rev. Mr Smeaton's sons, who had been educated at Loretto, where cricket was the game in the summer term, Tulliallan could boast of having an excellent cricket team. The Great War, when most young men were on active service, put an end to cricket in Tulliallan as in most parishes. In 1922, a move was made to resuscitate the game, but lack of equipment was the handicap. On 30th April a sale of work to provide the needed cash was opened by Sir Robert Maule, who recalled his membership of the team fifty years earlier and made a strong plea to the youth of the town, to take up, what he regarded as one of the finest summer sports. His visit that day to Tulliallan gave his friends the opportunity to present him and Lady Maule with a wedding gift which took the form of richly cut crystal table ware.

If Sir Robert kept in touch with his native town, no less did he keep in touch with his old school - Dollar Academy - to which he was generous in gifts as well as being an active member, and president of The Dollar Academy Club. It is not surprising then, that in 1922 he and Lady Maule - also a former pupil - were invited to be the chief guests of the annual exhibition and prize giving. He took occasion that day to give 100 guineas to the headmaster, to be used at his discretion for the benefit of the school. As a result, a six-valve wireless set, designed by Mr Howell, the science master, and constructed by members of the staff, capable of operating three loud speakers, was installed in the school. The principal duty of the chief guest was to deliver an address to the pupils and their parents. Sir Robert Maule's speech was long remembered. It was directed specifically to the pupils and in particular to the teenagers. Speaking of the industrial and commercial spheres, which he himself knew at first hand, he said that in them, the rewards for merit and competence, were greater than in any other. "If any of you go in for clerking, into a bank, or law office or a warehouse, don't be content to remain on the lower rungs of the ladder - 'aim high'." Stressing the need for educated men in commerce and business, if our nation were to hold its own in a highly competitive world, he urged his young hearers to make the most of what their school was offering them. "Hard work and thoroughness, will take you places; and whatever your work, at school or in later life, let your whole heart go into it."

But all work and no play makes Jack a dull boy - so, in a well-balanced life there must be recreation as well as work. Pointing out that, as a nation, we were entering on an ear of increasing leisure, he praised the value of good, clean sport and the importance of keeping physically fit - a subject on which, by the way, he was well qualified to speak, for he was not to know what a day's illness meant until three years later, when at the age of 73, he took a severe cold! He reminded his audience that wisdom's way was to preserve a right balance. The ancients spoke of a healthy mind in a healthy body. If leisure should be used to keep the body fit, it should no less be employed to enrich the mind. "Keep serious things in sight," he said, "cultivate the mind. Observe much and think more, always looking out for the best not in literature only but in life. Keep up your reading. There are plenty good books.

232

Be learners all your life. And one thing more, never forget that the kindly word and the helping hand are always needed - and will be always needed in a world like this. Do what good you can for your fellows and contribute a patriotic share to the building up of your country's life and prosperity." One is not surprised to read that his address was followed with close attention. It was simple. It was relevant. It appealed not to the base motives of human nature but to the noble. It came from the heart - for the speaker was enunciating his own philosophy of life. He was telling forth the things by which he himself had lived.

When they went to Leith, Robert and his parents joined the Se- cession Church - St Andrew's - where his father became an elder and he himself taught for several years in the Sunday School. Later, when he moved his home to Ravelston, he transferred to Inverleith Church where he served as an elder. But neither distance nor intervening years lessened his interest in St Andrew's Church, Leith. And when, about 1900, the congregation set out to raise £2,000 - a very large sum at that time - to defray the cost of a new organ, the renewal of the seating and the redecoration of their church it was Sir Robert Maule who opened their bazaar in the Music Hall in Edinburgh and by a substantial donation ensured its outstanding success. His generosity to the city of Edinburgh is seen in his paying, in 1917, the very considerable cost of the decoration of the frieze panels in the Council Chamber (Note 21).

In his later years Sir Robert spent much of his time at his country house at Tummel Bridge where he was a well-loved laird and neighbour. He enjoyed the magnificent scenery at all seasons of the year and in ideal conditions could follow his favourite recreations, angling and curling. He and Lady Maule were loyal members of the local United Free Church, which he had attended, when in residence at Dalreoch, for nearly thirty years. There, in June 1922, he placed a handsome memorial, in bronze, to the memory of his first wife who had died in 1914 and of their son, Lieutenant Robert Maule of the 5th Battalion of The Royal Scots, who fell in action in Gallipoli in 1915.

Sir Robert died at Dalreoch on 24th December 1931 in his 80th year. The funeral service in the church at Tummel Bridge was simple, as he would have desired. It was attended by the members of his family, his employees who were affectionately devoted to him, and a few neighbours. Thereafter, his remains were conveyed to Warriston Cemetery, Edinburgh, to be laid beside those of his parents and his first wife.

When he was in England in 1971, the Japanese Emperor paid a visit to Bertrand Russell, the mathematician and philosopher. In the course of conversation, Russell remarked: "Mine is only a small house". To which, with Royal courtesy, the Emperor replied, "It may be a small house but it contains a great man." Kincardine may be a small town, insignificant on a map, but it has been the birthplace of famous men:

SIR JAMES WYLIE - Surgeon to the three Czars of Russia, organiser of the Russian Army's medical service; founder of the Medical Colleges of Moscow and St Petersburgh.

SIR JAMES DEWAR - A prince of science, and

ROBERT MAULE and his son **SIR ROBERT** - co-founders and proprietors of a great commercial enterprise.

Notes

1.   Deed of Settlement by Robert Winchester, merchant, Kincardine, 24th May 1814. The four witnesses include John Maule, Taylor.

2.   The Clackmannan Advertiser, April 15th, 1848. The advertisement adds to the notice 'to let' that "another tenant in a similar line would be preferred but failing that, this would make an excellent opening for a watchmaker as there are none in the line nearer than Alloa".

3.   He married in 1850.

4.   Alloa Advertiser, March 16th, 1861: "House to let, entry at Whitsunday. The upper flat of that house situated in Toll Road, Kincardine, presently occupied by Mr Maule, draper. Apply to Captain Simpson."

5.   Ready-made clothing was being introduced into city shops about this time and endeavouring to capture the market from the tailor made-to-measure suits, etc., - which held a monopoly of advertisements in the Alloa Advertiser, The Scotsman, etc., in the 1850s. Maule's venture was something quite novel for a town such as Kincardine. Cf.

e.g. Alloa Advertiser, August 10th 1850. Advertisements by Peter Scott and Espie, South Bridge, Edinburgh.

6.   Cf. The Alloa Advertiser, 18th May, 1867. Some years earlier Robert Maule had commenced shawl weaving and his acquisition, in October, of the burnt out meal and

barley mill enabled him to extend his manufacturing activities. By October the fabric had been rebuilt, the requisite machinery installed and the premises had been turned into a weaving shed and a dyeing warehouse. He purchased the ground in September. - Sasine Records.

7.   Padella - a small vessel filled with fat or oil, in the centre of which a wick was placed, used for illuminations.

8.   The congregation of the United Presbyterian Church in Kincardine originated through members of Tulliallan Parish Church - the Established Church - becoming dissatisfied with the preaching and the doctrine taught by their minister. Desirous of obtaining teaching which was more evangelical they applied for 'pulpit supply' to The Associate (Burgher) Presbytery of Dunfermline in 1775; now forming themselves into a congregation of that denomination. Their first church was erected in 1777 and their first minister was the Rev. John Young from West Linton who was ordained on 19th March 1777. He remained at Kincardine for 30 years and was reputed to be fond of books and the fiddle, his fondness for the latter, of which he was an accomplished player, did not, we are told, meet with the approval of some of his elders. A second church was built in 1819 at the cost of £1,200 with accommodation for 750 people.

9.   The voting was 100 for the motion and 2 against.

10.   Thomas Buchanan was for many years Session Clerk of Tulliallan Parish Church and for thirty years the Superintendent of the Sunday School whose membership was always in excess of 200. He was the schoolmaster of the

Parish School which had a roll of over 100 pupils. Such was his ability and his skill as a teacher that the annual report of those who inspected the school was invariably most laudatory. The last years of his headmastership, following the appointment of School Boards in 1872, was rendered very unhappy by reason of the vendetta which was carried on against him inspired and led by the Rev. J. W. Laurie the minister of the Free Church. But Mr Buchanan retained the confidence and the respect of the vast majority of the parishioners of Tulliallan. He is buried in Alloa Cemetery.

11.   The principal reason for the economic decline of Kincardine in the nineteenth century is what we nowadays should describe as its inadequate infrastructure and in particular the absence of a train service for goods and passengers. Kincardine was completely by-passed by the railway system which had grown up all over the country. The nearest railway station was three miles distant. The steamboat service was altogether insufficient for a community which hoped to sustain its economy far less increase it. The Alloa Advertiser on February 15th, 1865 has this to say of the people of Kincardine: "They are great sufferers by being so far from the station and no steam boats are on the river during winter." At the social meeting in connection with the centenary of the United Presbyterian Church, the Rev. Mr Munro said of Kincardine that it was "shunted off from the great railway highways and the town has suffered most miserably. Trade has decline. The population has melted away till scarcely the ghost of its former life is seen amongst us." Such was the Kincardine which young Robert Maule urged

his father to leave in quest of an opportunity to build up a larger and more prosperous business.

12.   With his usual aplomb and flair for advertising Mr Maule set about the task of getting rid of Mr Ord's stock, offering to the citizens of Leith "unprecedented bargains". On 30th November his advertisement assured them that "all prices were marked plainly in red ink", and as a special inducement he had brought in from his own factory a selection of Scottish Clan Tartan plaids to be sold at 12 / 6, the usual price being 20 / -. In addition he had purchased a German manufacturer's stock of Winter Jackets, and as he was to do from time to time, he purchased the entire stock of a bankrupt manufacturer. With his uncanny discernment for what his prospective customers wanted he continued to buy good for which there was a huge demand with the result that in August 1873 when he and Robert staged their first summer sale they reported that over the three week period there had been constant overcrowding and apologised to their customers for not having been able to accord them the standard of service that was usual. Cf. The Leith Burgh Pilot, September 1873.

13.   James Taylor was a son of David Taylor, joiner, Hillhead, Tulliallan. His brother, Tom, joined The City of Edinburgh Police Force where he had a highly successful career as a detective.

14.   Sasine Records, October 31st, 1884.

15.   The architects were Baldie and Tennent, Glasgow. The contractors were: Fotheringham and Banningan, Stirling,

masons; Thomas Mitchell, Kincardine, joiner; Robert Frater, Stirling, plumber; William Dryburgh, Kincardine, slater; William Short, Kincardine, plasterer; R. Willison, Alloa Copper Works, ventilators.

16.   At the concert, which was attended by over 400 people, a poem, composed by a native of Kincardine in honour of the chairman, was read. It was as follows:

Well done, my friends, Kincardine has at length
Made an advance upon the things that were,
A waste unsightly once, is now reclaimed
And on its site an adifice now stands
Which shall proclaim to all around that love
Still holds a place on earth, that hearts are still
Found in our clime, that from a fountain head
Unsealed, pour forth perennial streams whose power
Is felt, and the parched places in men's heads
Are watered, as with dew of heaven's own store
Drop after drop makes up the genial shower
Whose influence tells upon the arid plain;
Makes roses bloom, refreshes nature's face
That she rejoices with a gladsome sound;
While on the early boughs the forest train
Pour forth their harmony to show that they
Are not unthankful for the blessing given.
He built us hath a synagogue, he loves
Our nation, and is worthy to receive
A blessing: so in days of old men pled
For one, who was an alien to their race,
But yet had by his deeds of love, aroused

Within their souls those strong desires, that he
Might get the gift of life from Heaven's Great King
And that his soul might be refreshed with grace
And that his loved ones too might get a share;
But he who holds the honoured place tonight
Is not a stranger, nay! he's one of ourselves
He knows us one by one and on our hearts
His image is inscribed by deeds of love.
We gladly give him welcome but will not
Descend to flatter. That love cannot do.
But yet she speaks true words from out the heart
And cares not who may call them praise, she knows
So does pure love reflect an image true.
We give him kinder welcome, in these days
When some would say that men of wealth have hearts
Yet feel not for their neighbours, nor respond
Unto the cry for help, the poor upraise;
But our true, tried and much respected friend
Knows the full meaning of those gracious words;
"It is more blessed to bestow than get"
For he that scatters with a bounteous hand
His store doth still increase: he feels that some
Touched in a tender part, pray oft for him
In earnest tones; that God would bless him still
And as He hath bestowed the gift of wealth
And heart to give, so many He make him one
Of His, and may his house that promise take
And make it theirs; the righteous ne'er shall be
Forsaken, and his seed beg for their bread."
And when life's cares and joys shall be fulfilled
May he and they receive the welcome mead

And hear the loving Father say - "Well done".

The poet was probably Andrew Crocket.

17.   Another innovation, introduced some years later, was the paying of tramway fares for the Edinburgh customers who, at sale times, could go to the office in the shop and obtain a voucher for their tram fare home.

18.   The Courant Fund was established in 1883 by Mr William Anderson to provide for the poor children of the city of Edinburgh a day's outing to the country and a treat at Christmas. Robert Maule (Jr) became keenly interested and after serving on the Committee responsible for raising funds and organising the events he was elected chairman on 23rd December 1918. In the late 1920s unemployment was widespread as was also poverty and destitution in the city. The summer outings usually took place to Norton Park, Ratho, whither the children were conveyed by train on each of the three or four days, some 1500 travelling on each excursion. At Christmas the children were, with the willing and generous co-operation of the cinema proprietors, entertained to a free cinema show and on leaving received a bag containing cakes, fruit - usually and orange - and sweets. The year 1925 is typical. That year 7,000 poor children were given a day's outing to Ratho, where ample catering and games were enjoyed. 10,000 were entertained in the various cinemas at the festive season. Sir Robert and Lady Maule were assiduous in visiting all the events and when during the war and afterwards the cost often outran the income from donations this good man said that he would guarantee to make

up any deficit incurred rather than see any child forfeit the picnic at Ratho or the Christmas treat. As chairman Sir Robert, with Lady Maule, usually entertained all the voluntary helpers at the picnics to tea in his restaurant in Princes Street. Cf. Minutes of The Courant Fund.

19.   On the evening of Friday, 30th September 1904, a 'house warming' party took place at Dalreoch Lodge nestling under the shadow of Schiehallion at which two hundred guests, including many from the neighbourhood, at- tended. The commodious and handsomely furnished lodge was lit by electricity derived from a turbine on the river Tummel. The gardens, as befitted a Swiss type chalet, were laid out by Sir Robert's Swiss gardener. For this special occasion the house and gardens were beautifully illuminated by coloured fairy lights and Japanese lanterns. Dancing took place in a large marquee in which a comfortable wooden floor was installed and music was provided by a band from Edinburgh and a piper from Aberfeldy.

20.   ii Kings VI v. 30

21.   This notable frieze which was presented by Sir Robert Maule and was designed by Mr Dobie, enhances greatly the beauty of a very attractive room. Sir Robert stipulated that the emblem of the thistle should be introduced with the coat of arms of the consorts of the monarchs from Malcolm Canmore down to the time of the union of the crowns. The space above the gallery contains a shield with the St Andrew's cross as an appropriate centre piece. The panel above the fireplace contains the old Scottish arms of the monarch. Altogether it

was a very appropriate and handsome benefaction to the city of his adoption.
